He Says, She Says

He Says, She Says

CLOSING THE COMMUNICATION GAP BETWEEN THE SEXES

Dr. Lillian Glass

PIATKUS

To the greatest woman I know,
my mother
Rosalie Glass

For her many talents, enormous strength and
wisdom, for her overcoming some of life's most
difficult obstacles yet always maintaining her
dignity, elegance and loveliness, for her warmth
and tenderness, for her upbeat and positive
attitude and for always loving me and being
there for me – no matter what.
I am truly blessed.
Mom, I love you.

Copyright © 1992 by Lillian Glass
This edition first published in
Great Britain in 1992 by
Judy Piatkus (Publishers) Ltd of
5 Windmill Street, London W1

The moral right of the author has been asserted

*A catalogue record for this book
is available from the British Library*
ISBN 0-7499-1200-6 hardback
ISBN 0-7499-1207-3 paperback

Designed by Sue Ryall
Cover design by Ken Leeder

Set in 11/13pt Linotron Baskerville by
Computerset, Harmondsworth, Middlesex
Printed and bound in Great Britain by
Biddles Ltd, Guildford & King's Lynn

Contents

Acknowledgements   vi

Introduction   vii

1 Sex Talk Quiz   1

2 What Are These Sex Talk Differences?   14

3 The Evolution of Sex Differences
in Communication   29

4 Improving Your Personal and Social
Relationships with the Opposite Sex   40

5 Closing the Communication Gap in
Your Intimate Relationships   86

6 Closing the Communication Gap at Work   134

7 Closing the Communication Gap for Good   172

Source List   179

Index   189

Acknowledgements

I wish to thank the following people for their support and kindness in completion of this book: my agent and attorney Susan Grode, John Benson of the Roper Organization, John McNei of the Gallup Organization, Dr Burt Crausman, Dr Howard Flaks, Dr Anthony Johnson, my mentor Dr H. Harlan Bloomer, Dustin Hoffman, my father Anthony A. Glass, my brother Joseph M. Glass, Lamie Glass, Suzie W. Yoon, Neeria Maggio, Dale Alan Neff, and all of my clients and friends throughout the years who have helped provide the basis for this book.

Introduction

One out of every two marriages ends in divorce

One of the biggest fears of adults in the Western world today is the fear of intimate communication. Several studies have shown that the divorce rate is high because people seem to be more willing to leave a relationship than to get to the root of the problem through honest and open communication.

Extramarital affairs among married men and married women are at a peak

People want to be with someone they can talk to and who will listen to them. Often couples will not leave a marriage but have extramarital affairs instead. Usually it is not a new sexual relationship that couples are longing for, but rather the closeness of someone who will listen to them, who will understand them and who will talk to them. If couples would learn how to communicate better with one another by using what I call the SEX TALK RULES – the do's and don't's of how to communicate with the opposite sex – there would be virtually no need to look for someone else.

The rate of sexual dysfunction for both men and women has dramatically increased over the last five years

Psychologists feel that poor communication skills are to blame for this. Understanding and incorporating the SEX TALK RULES can also enhance intimacy between couples. Most marriage and sex counsellors believe that the major cause of impotence in males and of frigidity in females is that couples do not know how to communicate their desires openly and honestly. Often it is not only the words they use but also the tones they use that alienate, cause emptiness and even result in hostility. By learning how to utilize SEX TALK RULES couples can sidestep or eliminate these problems.

Women complain of not advancing rapidly enough in business

Poor communication skills may have a great deal to do with that. If a grown woman has a little girl's high-pitched vocal tones, insecure body language and an inability to communicate with her male colleagues, these can all inhibit her chances of rising up the corporate ladder.

Many men and women do not realize that they themselves may be contributing to their own sexual harassment

Subliminal suggestions may frequently be due to poor communication skills with members of the opposite sex. Applying the SEX TALK RULES to job situations can solve a

Applying the SEX TALK RULES to job situations can solve a variety of work-related problems and reduce the odds of your being the victim of sexual harassment. For example, inappropriate laughter and vocal inflections can be seen as encouragement to sexual advances. All too often, women do not advance in the workforce because they have not learned how to use the SEX TALK RULES to their advantage.

The fact that many men and women continue to communicate in sexual stereotypes perpetuates in our society today all the problems mentioned above. The way in which both men and women have been raised, conditioned and socialized has created genuine and sometimes even insurmountable communication problems for both sexes. We take it for granted that the opposite sex understands us, yet it has clearly been proven by the frustration of miscommunication between the sexes that men and women do not communicate in similar ways.

When I first began studying sex differences in communication I found it to be a tangled string. However, my experiences and those of my many clients have helped me to untangle it, and throughout this book I will share my conclusions with you.

My interest in this topic was sparked while working on my master's degree at the University of Michigan in Ann Arbor. My mentor, Dr H. Harlan Bloomer, one of the founding fathers of the field of speech pathology, asked me to diagnose a patient he was seeing. As an ambitious young student I embarked on an elaborate analysis of the vocal and speech characteristics of this extremely attractive black woman who spoke with a somewhat low-pitched voice. Although my diagnosis of her voice quality was correct, I was completely unaware that the woman I was evaluating was actually a man – a transsexual who was undergoing hormonal treatment. Because of my curiosity about this patient and my desire to help her sound and act like a woman, I read all the scientific literature I could get my hands on that had anything to do with differences in communication between men and women. But in the mid-1970s not much was available with the exception of linguist Robin Lakoff's research and her classic book *Language and Women's Place*.

Five years later, in 1980, while doing post-doctorate research in medical genetics at UCLA School of Medicine, I received a call from a Hollywood producer who asked me if I knew anything about male and female differences in communication. He asked me if I could help make a male actor sound like a woman.

I told the producer about my experience with the transsexual patient and proceeded to quote some of the scientific literature citing some of the specific sex differences between men and women. He then asked me to meet him and the actor in a rather clandestine fashion. The actor turned out to be Dustin Hoffman. The film they were working on was, of course, the enormously popular *Tootsie*, in which Dustin portrayed a woman so brilliantly that he won an Academy Award for his performance.

While gathering up all the scientific research I needed to share with Dustin Hoffman, I became intrigued by how incredibly different men and women were, especially in terms of how they talked to one another. For example, when analyzing Dustin's performances in earlier films I could see how masculine he was in terms of body language and verbal communication. In the film *Kramer vs. Kramer* his 'maleness' was vividly depicted: he hardly opened his mouth, nor did he use his facial muscles to create animation or emotion. He had a monotonous tone – a drone with no life in it – as he tried to express meaning in what he said. There was little or no inflection or intonation, and he left endings off words (comin', goin'). He would answer questions with one-word responses such as 'Yup' or 'Nope', and he had abrupt physical movements. These typical 'male' communication patterns certainly could not have created effective verbal understanding between the character of 'Mr Kramer' and Meryl Streep's Mrs Kramer, the wife who was leaving him. So it came as no surprise that the two characters in the movie finalized their separation by divorce.

These SEX TALK DIFFERENCES can be clearly seen in *Tootsie* when one begins to analyze how vastly different the two characters – Michael Dorsey (Dustin as the male) and Dorothy Michaels (Dustin as the female) – appear to be.

In the scene where Dustin (as Michael) is in his agent's office, he is abrupt in his physical movements and vocal tones. His movements are angular, broad and away from his body, while his legs are spread apart when he sits down. In essence, it takes up more room. His speech is faster, more clipped and staccato, and even more nasal, since he barely opens his mouth or his lips when he speaks. He uses hardly any facial animation, even though his most openly expressed emotions appear to be anger and hostility as a result of his frustration at being unable to get work as a 'male' actor.

In contrast, recall the scene in the Russian Tea Room when Hoffman, as Dorothy, first enters to meet 'her' agent. Her gestures are more delicate, smaller and directed towards her body. When she speaks she puts her hand on her upper chest, smiles more and uses more facial animation, which makes her appear to be more receptive and acquiescent. She uses a soft, breathier voice with upward inflection at the end as she declares: 'I will have a Dubonnet on the rocks with a twist.' This upward inflection makes her statement sound as though she is asking a question. It is an all-too-common female communication pattern which may often give the illusion that the woman is tentative, weak, unsure of herself or even a helpless victim.

After Dustin Hoffman, I worked with numerous other male performers in Hollywood who were cast to portray female roles. Conrad Bain, star of the television situation comedy *Different Strokes*, was one of these. While working with Conrad I was presented with an even greater challenge: I not only had to teach him how to sound female but how to sound like a Dutch female – accent and all. In addition I had to teach his female co-star, Dana Plato, who played the role of his daughter Kimberly, how to speak and behave like a boy – a Dutch boy complete with accent – for her sex role reversal in that particular show.

After these experiences had brought the subject into focus for me I began to realize that it was no accident that so many marriages failed, or that so many people had difficulty dealing with opposite-sex colleagues in the workplace. I began to see various patterns emerging – these were the culprits for the continuing conflicts between men and women. In essence, I stumbled upon a secret that needed to be shared with everyone.

As a result, I gave numerous television and radio interviews around the world and delivered several lectures and seminars about the subject. My views on communication differences also appeared in newspaper and magazine articles in many countries. I even found myself quoted in Steven Naifeh and Gregory Smith's book *Why Can't Men Open Up?*, where they discussed my work in the area of sex differences and communication.

My interest in the subject evolved further while working with clients in my private practice in Beverley Hills, where I continued to hear many similar problems and concerns. Although the names, places and circumstances were different, the bottom line was the same – men and women really don't know how to talk to one another.

Although thousands of different scenarios were described to me, I began to see common threads running through them. For example, many women whom I listened to did not realize that their beating around the bush and not getting to the point at a business meeting was a typically female communication pattern which would often elicit a negative response from male colleagues and prevent them from gaining professional respect. In contrast, many of my male clients were generally not aware that their direct commands and lack of descriptive adjectives when talking to their wives and girlfriends had a bad effect on their relationships with women.

My advice usually produced amazing results in my clients. One woman, for instance, noticed that her predominantly male colleagues shuffled papers and looked inattentive during her early morning business presentations. When she showed me her presentation I saw that it was not concise – rather, it was very detailed and went off on various tangents. I suggested that, when she had to make her next presentation the following month, she should first state what the bottom line was. This would allow her to get to the point. Then she should enumerate the other points of discussion, address these issues systematically and unemotionally, and finally ask if anyone had any questions. She took my advice, and was astounded at the outcome. For the very first time in her professional life, she noticed that her audience of men actually paid attention to what she had to say.

I told one male client to tell his wife *why* she looked beautiful, and specifically describe how he felt about her, instead of simply saying 'You look nice.' He noticed that his wife showed more warmth and suddenly became more affectionate and loving towards him.

My observations also inspired me to mention these differences in the way men and women communicate in my book *Confident Conversation: How to Talk in Any Business or Social Situation*. The chapter called 'Sweet Talk' discussed how to talk to your partner, and those who read it were anxious to learn more about the subject. People wrote me letters from all over the world and even asked me questions about it during my seminars. They weren't satisfied just to know that sex differences existed – they wanted me to tell them exactly what to do, in other words how to handle their particular situations.

This book lists all these male and female communication differences and offers a practical plan of action to improve relations between the sexes. It addresses male–female communication in broad terms by discussing the many different aspects of communication, ranging from body language through facial language, speech voice patterns and language content to behaviour patterns. This adds up to 105 SEX TALK DIFFERENCES.

Chapters 1–3 describe these differences in a comprehensive, organized and easy-to-read manner. These chapters are peppered with case studies to which most readers will be able to relate.

Chapters 4–6 list the SEX TALK DIFFERENCES relevant to the respective chapters and tell you exactly what to do and how to incorporate this knowledge into your personal life, during sex and at work. At the end of these chapters you will find a list of the SEX TALK RULES which men and women need to follow in order to close the communication gap between the sexes in these three major areas of their lives.

He Says, She Says is the book of the nineties that can and will change your personal life, your love life and your business life for the better. It is a practical guide to help you become a better lover, mate, social partner and business associate with the other half of the population. By learning to communicate with sensitivity towards the opposite sex you will achieve a richer, less stressful, more eventful and, in general, happier life. By freeing you from the problems stemming from stereotyped behaviour this book will also help you to raise a new generation of people who are more at ease and more successful at communicating with one another, which in turn will make for a better world.

Like anything else you learn to do well, the SEX TALK RULES need to be practised. If you do so, they are guaranteed to help you overcome communication blocks and close the communication gap with the opposite sex forever.

Dr Lillian Glass

1

Sex Talk Quiz

How well do you know the opposite sex? This SEX TALK QUIZ is designed to show how much you really know about the way men and women communicate. The questions and answers originated from various studies in scientific books and periodicals regarding sex differences in communication, as well as from data obtained via surveys and polls such as Gallup Poll.

Here are twenty-five statements. Put a tick in the TRUE column on the left to indicate the the ones with which you agree, and put a tick in the FALSE column on the right for those with which you disagree. Then turn to the answers on p. 4 to discover how well you know the opposite sex.

SEX TALK QUIZ

	TRUE	FALSE

1 Women are more intuitive than men. They have a sixth sense which is termed 'feminine intuition'. — —

2 At business meetings colleagues are more likely to listen to men than they are to women. — —

3 Women are the 'talkers'. In group conversations they talk much more than men. — —

4 Men are the 'fast talkers' – they talk much faster than women. — —

5 Men are more outwardly open than women. They use more eye contact and exhibit more friendliness when first meeting someone. — —

6 Women are more complimentary: they give more praise than men do. — —

7 Men interrupt more than women do and will even answer a question when it is not addressed to them. — —

8 Women give more orders than men and are more demanding in the way they communicate. — —

2

TRUE FALSE

9 In general, men and women laugh at the same things. — —

10 When making love, both men and women want to hear the same things from their partner. — —

11 Men ask for assistance less often than women do. — —

12 Men are harder on themselves and blame themselves more often than women do. — —

13 Through their body language women make themselves less confrontational than men. — —

14 Men tend to explain things in greater detail than women when discussing an incident. — —

15 Women tend to touch others more often than men do. — —

16 Men appear to be more attentive than women when they are listening. — —

17 Women and men are equally emotional when they speak. — —

18 Men are more likely than women to discuss personal issues. — —

3

TRUE   FALSE

19   Men bring up more topics of
conversation than women do.   — | —

20   Today, we tend to bring up boys in
the same way as girls.   — | —

21   Women tend to confront problems
more directly than men and are likely
to bring up any problem first.   — | —

22   Men are livelier speakers than
women; they use more body language
and facial animation.   — | —

23   Men ask more questions than
women.   — | —

24   In general, men and women enjoy
talking about similar things.   — | —

25   A woman is more likely than a
man to bring up the topics of safe sex
or whether the partner has had an
HIV test.   — | —

ANSWERS

1 FALSE. According to studies there is no truth in the
myth that women are more intuitive than men. However,
according to world-renowned anthropologist Ashley
Montagu, women do have greater sensitivity than men
when differentiating between colours, as he mentions in

4

his book *The Natural Superiority of Women*. In *Language and Women's Place* Robin Lakoff confirms this, stating that women tend to be more descriptive and to use finer discrimination between colours than men do. For instance, women will use words like 'cinnabar', 'bone', 'coral' and 'ebony'.

Studies have also shown that women are conditioned to pay greater attention to detail than men. Thus women appear to be more intuitive because they tend to be more sensitive and to pay greater attention to a person's body language, vocal tones and facial expressions. In early childhood baby girls seem to be more aware of parents' and others' facial expressions than baby boys are. This may be carried over into adulthood and explain why women can often perceive a person's mood and emotional state better than men can. As a result of their conditioning, women have also been found to be more sensitive to non-verbal communication than men, which also makes them appear to be more intuitive.

2   TRUE. Men are listened to more often than women are. In their study entitled 'Sex Differences in Listening Comprehension', Kenneth Gruber and Jacqueline Gaehelein found that both male and female audiences tended to listen more attentively to male speakers than they did to female ones. Audiences also tended to remember more information from a presentation given by a male speaker, even when that presentation was identical to one made by a woman. Another study showed that at a scientific conference there was less noise in the room – audiences talking or shuffling papers – when men spoke than when women spoke. One possible explanation relates to voice control and vocal pitch. A high-pitched, little-girl voice tends to turn an audience off and prevent them from hearing the information being presented.

3 FALSE. Contrary to popular stereotype, it is men –
not women – who talk more. Studies like the one done by
linguist Lynette Hirschman in 1974 show that men far out-
talk women. In fact women tend to ask more questions,
while men tend to give more answers, which are lengthier
and more involved than the questions they are asked. One
study found that when asked to describe a painting, women only spoke on average for three minutes while men
averaged thirteen minutes. Several studies, from Fred
Strodtbeck's in 1951 via Marion Wood's in 1966 to Marjorie Swacker's in 1975, confirm that women speak less
than men in mixed-sex conversations.

4 FALSE. Although women talk at a more rapid rate,
that does not necessarily mean that women talk extremely
fast. It is just that women tend to articulate more precisely
and more quickly than men. Perhaps this is due to the fact
that men tend to interrupt more, so that women hurry to
get out all their information before they are interrupted.

5 FALSE. It is women and not men who tend to maintain eye contact and facial pleasantries. A study by Dr
Albert Merhabian showed that in positive interactions
women increased their eye contact, while men tended to be
more uncomfortable and in essence to decrease their eye
contact. Other studies by Merhabian, as well as Dr Nancy
Henley in the chapter entitled 'Power, Sex, and Non-
Verbal Communication' in her book *Language and Sex:
Difference and Dominance*, show that women exhibit more
friendly behaviour such as smiles, facial pleasantries and
head nods than men do. This is especially true when first
meeting someone. Research indicates that, even though
women were found to smile 93 per cent of the time, only
about 57 per cent of their smiles were returned by men.

6 TRUE. Women are more open in their praise and
give more nods of approval than men. Throughout their

speech they also use more complimentary terms, according to *Word-Play: What Happens When People Talk* by Peter Farb, who studied the vocabulary of men and women. Robin Lakoff found that during conversational speech women tend to interject more 'uhm mmm's' as an indicator of approval when listening to members of either sex.

7 TRUE. In 1975, at the University of California, researchers Donald Zimmerman and Candace West conducted a study on how often interruptions occurred when men and women conversed. Their results showed that from 75-93 per cent of the interruptions were made by men. In another study, of eleven conversations between men and women, there was only one where the woman interrupted the man, but there were ten where the man interrupted the woman. After being interrupted by the man, the woman often became increasingly quiet and paused more than normal after starting to speak again. Dr Zimmerman and Dr West believe that the reason men tend to interrupt is that it may be a way of establishing dominance. This conversational 'dominance' is also verified in Judy Kester's 1978 observations, which found that men are more likely than women to answer questions that are not even addressed to them.

8 FALSE. It is the men who use more command terms or imperatives, which makes them sound more demanding. In essence, several researchers have concluded that women tend to be more polite in their speech. According to the University of California's Mary Ritchie Key, an expert on women's speech, women tend to be more 'tentative' when they speak. This is because they generally communicate from a position where they are not the decision-makers – men are. In *Language and Women's Place* Robin Lakoff reveals her classic discovery of women's use of 'tag endings' – asking a question after a declarative statement is made, such as 'It's a nice day, *isn't it?*' This adds

7

to the image of women appearing to be more tentative in their conversation and less sure of themselves. She also found that women are less likely to make use of command terms, but will often appear to command with terms of politeness or endearment such as 'Darling, would you mind closing the door?' The more direct 'Close the door', is a typical command that a man will use without even thinking about it. This may be conditioned early in childhood, as shown by researchers Daniel Maltz and Ruth Borker's *A Cultural Approach to Male–Female Miscommunication in Language and Social Identity*. They contend that little boys and girls differ in the way they talk to their friends. Little girls don't give orders like boys, who will say, 'Give me that' or 'Get out of here.' Instead, girls tend to use suggestions in order to express themselves such as 'How about doing that' or 'Let's do this.'

9 FALSE. Men and women definitely differ in their sense of humour. According to researcher Carol Mitchell's 1985 study 'Some Differences in Male-Female Joke Telling', women are more likely to tell jokes when there is a small, non-mixed-sex group, while men are even more likely to tell jokes in a larger mixed-sex group. Both Robin Lakoff and Nancy Henley discovered that women tell jokes less frequently than men. Psychologist Paul McGhee's 1979 research indicates that male humour tends to be more hostile, abrasive and sarcastic than women's. Men also tend to joke around with one another as a 'bonding' technique or to establish camaraderie with one another, according to Robin Lakoff, while women don't use jokes in this way.

10 FALSE. In a survey which I conducted for the Playboy Channel in the USA, people were asked what they wanted to hear when making love. In general, women wanted to be told they were beautiful and loved, while men wanted to hear how good they were in bed and how they pleased their women. In a recent Gallup Poll commissioned for this book, I found that only 30 per cent of the men and women surveyed were pleased with what they heard from the opposite sex while making love. Fewer women than men were found to like what was being said to them in bed.

11 TRUE. In her book *You Just Don't Understand: Women and Men in Conversation* Deborah Tannen found that men will not usually ask for help by asking for directions, while women will. She attributes this to the fact that men are usually givers of information, while women are takers. As givers, men are proclaimed the experts and superiors in knowledge, while women are considered uninformed and inferior.

12 FALSE. Several surveys and numerous psychotherapists' observations show that women are in general more self-critical and apt to blame themselves than men are. Women tend to be more self-deprecating and apologetic when things go wrong. They also often personalize a problem, take responsibility for it or blame themselves when they may not even have instigated it. Deborah Tannen's findings confirm this as she states that women are also disposed to use more 'apologetic phrases' in their conversations, such as 'I'm sorry' or 'I didn't mean to'.

13 TRUE. The great naturalist Charles Darwin stated that making oneself appear smaller by bowing the head to take up less space can inhibit human aggression. This observation is supported by the research of Ray Birdwhistell (1970), Albert Merhabian (1972) and Marguerite Piercy (1973), who found that women frequently inhibit themselves by crossing their legs at the ankles or knees or keeping their elbows by their sides. Since women take up less room in their body language, they make themselves less available for confrontation than men. This body language reflects less power and status.

14 FALSE. Women are in general more detailed and more descriptive than men in what they say and in how they explain things. As Robin Lakoff's research shows, women use more description in word choices. They describe things in greater detail by their use of certain adjectives and intensifiers such as 'so', 'vastly' and 'immensely'. Observations of male–female communication patterns also indicate that women speak less in concise statements. They prefer to go into greater detail about an incident than men would, which often sidetracks the conversation. This is substantiated in a survey which I conducted for this book; it indicated that men are most frustrated by women going on and on, beating around the bush and not getting to the point quickly enough.

15 FALSE. Men tend to touch more than females. According to several researchers such as Stanley Jourard, Jane Rubin, and Barbara and Gene Eakins, women are more likely to be physically touched by men who guide them through doors, assist them with coats and help them into cars. Nancy Henley's research substantiates these findings. Her study showed that in a variety of outdoor settings men touched women four times as much as women touched men. Men have also been shown to touch one another more (for instance, back slapping and handshakes) while participating in various sports than women touch one another.

16 FALSE. Women, not men, appear to be more attentive when listening. Studies consistently show that women exhibit greater eye contact and express approval by smiling and nodding their heads as a form of attentiveness and agreement. Sally McConnell-Ginetts' research at Cornell University found that, when listening to another person

10

speak, women are more inclined to say 'uhm-mmm' than men in order to monitor the 'connectedness' of the conversation.

17 TRUE. Men and women are equally emotional when they speak. However, women appear to *sound* more emotional, according to researchers such as Robin Lakoff, because they use more psychological state verbs – for instance, 'I feel', 'I think', 'I hope' and 'I wish'. Women also have a greater variety of vocal intonation patterns. Nancy Henley and Barrie Thorne's 1975 research, as well as that done by Robert Luchsinger and Geoffrey Arnold, showed that women use approximately five tones when expressing themselves while men only use three. This makes them sound more monotonous and unemotional than women. In addition, men have been observed to express their emotions through increased vocal intensity – for instance loudness, shouting or swear words. Women, on the other hand, express themselves by getting quieter, speaking in a shaky voice quality or starting to cry.

18 FALSE. In general men bring up fewer personal topics than women do. Women like to bring up topics about people, relationships, children, self-improvement and how certain experiences have affected them. Men prefer to be more 'outer directed' as they originate discussions about events, news, sports-related issues, and topics that bear on more concrete physical tasks.

19 FALSE. Even though men do not bring up as many subjects of conversation as women, men interrupt more, which ultimately gives them control of the topics which are raised by women. Research by Don Zimmerman and Candace West, and a study done by Pam Fishman of Queen's College in New York, verified this finding. Ms Fishman discovered that over 60 per cent of the topics introduced into conversation were broached by women. However, even though women introduced subjects more often, this may have been because men tended to interrupt more, thus making the conversation change continually.

20 FALSE. Even though there are many progressive and socially enlightened parents, some parents still treat boys different from girls. They tend to communicate differently to their children according to their sex, which in turn induces sex-stereotyped behaviour. For example, a recent Harvard University study showed that mothers tended to be more verbal towards their daughters than towards their sons. Current studies have also shown that boy babies are handled more physically and robustly, and are spoken to in louder tones, than girl babies.

21 TRUE. Even though men tend to make more direct statements, a survey I conducted for this book indicated that women confront and bring up a problem more often than men. In a survey of a hundred men and women between the ages of eighteen and sixty-five, over 70 per cent of the women stated that they would be the ones to confront a problem while only about 40 per cent of men claimed that they would make the first move. Even though women bring up a problem more often, they tend to be more indirect and polite as Deborah Tannen relates in her book. This can also be seen in the Gallup Poll results, which reveal that women are more likely than men to confront issues such as AIDS, sexually transmitted diseases and safe sex.

22 FALSE. According to anthropologists at the University of California at San Francisco, women are more facially animated than men when speaking. Studies also show that women make more eye contact, use more body movement and intonation, have a more varied pitch range, and use more emotionally laden words and phrases than men.

12

23   FALSE. Just as women bring up more topics of con-
.versation, they also ask more questions. This is usually
done to facilitate the conversation.

24   FALSE. Men and women usually talk about different
things. Women enjoy talking about diet, personal relationships, personal appearance, clothes, self-improvement,
children, marriages, the personalities of others, the actions of others, relationships at work and emotionally
charged issues that have a personal component. Men, on
the other hand, enjoy discussing sports, what they did at
work, where they went, news events, mechanical gadgets,
the latest technology, cars, vehicles and music.

25   TRUE. In a recent Gallup Poll survey commissioned
for this book, it was found that women were more likely
than men to bring up the topic of AIDS testing and safe
sex.

If you got any of these questions wrong you need to
continue reading this book. Unfortunately, too many people have developed stereotypes, misconceptions and
preconceived notions about how the opposite sex communicates. Because of this they find themselves at a
disadvantage when talking to their spouses, lovers, friends
and even business associates of the opposite sex.

2

What Are These Sex Talk Differences?

When discussing the actual communication differences between men and women, many people say, 'No – not me. I don't do that. I don't act that way.' Maybe *you* don't. Maybe *you* behave differently because of the way you have been socialized or because of your social expectations and lifestyle. True, it is unfair to compare the communication skills of a female executive in a major company with that of a male childcare worker. As women achieve more success up the corporate ladder, and men take more and more responsibility for child rearing and become more sensitive to the ways they communicate, these differences will in many instances balance out. However, like it or not, basic sex differences do exist. In fact, using the research available, I have compiled 105 such differences which are clearly laid out below. The results of the differences are based on the scientific work of linguists, psychologists, speech pathologists, anthropologists and communication specialists listed on p. 179.

BODY LANGUAGE

MEN	WOMEN
1 They take up more physical space when sitting or standing, with arms and legs stretched out away from their body.	**1** They take up less physical space when sitting, with arms and legs towards their body.
2 Their gestures are more forceful, angular and restricted.	**2** Their gestures are more fluid, easy and light.
3 They gesture away from the body.	**3** They gesture towards the body.
4 They gesture with their fingers together, or they point their fingers.	**4** They gesture with their fingers apart and use curved hand movements.
5 They assume more reclined positions when sitting, and lean backward when listening.	**5** They assume more forward positions when sitting, and lean forward when listening.
6 They use their arms independently from the trunk of their bodies.	**6** They move their entire bodies from their necks to their ankles.
7 They provide less listener feedback through their body language.	**7** They provide more listener feedback through their body language.

MEN	WOMEN
8 They are not as sensitive to the communication cues of others.	**8** They have greater sensitivity towards other people's non-verbal communication cues.
9 They invade other people's body space more often.	**9** They invade other people's body space less often.
10 In general, they touch others more often.	**10** They touch others less often.
11 They are touched less often by women.	**11** They are touched more often by men.
12 They are less gentle when touching others. (i.e. back slapping, crushing handshakes).	**12** They are more gentle when touching others (i.e. fondling and caressing).
13 They have a stronger handshake grip.	**13** They have a weaker handshake grip.
14 They fidget and shift their body position more.	**14** They fidget and shift their body position less.
15 They move round the room more when giving a speech.	**15** They move around the room less when giving a speech.
16 They sit more at an angle and further apart from the other person, especially women.	**16** They sit directly in front of the other person and sit closer to men.

MEN	WOMEN
17 They tend to approach women more closely in terms of their personal space.	**17** They do not approach men as closely in terms of their personal space.
18 They do not move out of women's way and do not walk round them when approaching them.	**18** They tend to walk round men or move out of their way when approaching them.
19 They sit further away from women.	**19** They sit closer to men.

FACIAL LANGUAGE

20 They tend to avoid eye contact and do not look directly at the other person.	**20** They look more directly at another person and have better eye contact.
21 They tend to cock their head to the side and look at the other person from an angle when listening to a conversation.	**21** They tend to look at the other person directly, with their heads and eyes facing forward, when listening.
22 They tend to frown and squint when listening.	**22** They smile and nod their head when listening.
23 They provide fewer facial expressions in feedback and fewer reactions.	**23** They provide more facial expressions in feedback and more reactions.

17

MEN	WOMEN
24 They exhibit less emotional warmth through facial animation.	**24** They exhibit more emotional warmth through facial animation.
25 They open their jaw less when speaking.	**25** They open their jaw more when speaking.
26 They stare more in negative interaction (i.e. when angry or upset).	**26** They lower their eyes more to avert gaze in negative interaction (i.e. when angry or upset).
27 They use little eye contact in positive interaction (i.e. when pleased or happy).	**27** They use more eye contact in positive interaction (i.e. when pleased or happy).

SPEECH AND VOICE PATTERNS

28 They interrupt others more, and allow fewer interruptions.	**28** They interrupt others less, and allow more interruptions.
29 They use more fillers ('like', 'um', 'uh') during conversational speech.	**29** They use fewer fillers ('like', 'um', 'uh') during conversational speech.
30 They mumble words more and have sloppier pronunciation.	**30** They use quicker and more precise articulation and better pronunciation.
31 They sound more nasal due to not opening their jaw more.	**31** They sound less nasal due to opening their jaw more.

MEN	WOMEN
32 They are more likely to leave off 'ng' sounds from words (e.g. 'comin'' and 'goin'').	**32** They are more likely to include 'ng' sounds in words (e.g. 'coming' and 'going').
33 They use less intonation and vocal inflection.	**33** They use more intonation and vocal inflection.
34 They have more monotonous speech. They use approximately three tones when talking.	**34** They sound more 'emotional'. They use approximately five tones when talking.
35 They have a lower-pitched voice and show less tendency to have a child-like voice.	**35** They have a higher-pitched voice and show more tendency to have a high, child-like voice.
36 They speak in a louder voice.	**36** They speak in a softer voice.
37 They use more choppy and staccato tones. They sound more abrupt and less approachable.	**37** They use more flowing tones. They sound less abrupt and more approachable.
38 They use loudness to emphasize points.	**38** They use pitch and inflection to emphasize points.
39 They talk at a slower rate.	**39** They talk at a faster rate.
40 They use fewer soft and breathy tones.	**40** They use more soft and breathy tones.

MEN	WOMEN
41 They talk more and monopolize the conversation. They talk about things and activities such as cars, sports, jobs and mechanical objects.	**41** They talk less. They talk about people, relationships, clothes, diets, feelings and children.
42 They disclose less personal information about themselves.	**42** They disclose more personal information about themselves.
43 They refer to basic description of colours (e.g. green and blue).	**43** They use finer discrimination in description of colour (e.g. indigo, chartreuse, bone).
44 They make direct accusations (e.g. 'You don't call').	**44** They make more indirect accusations. They use 'why' in accusations, which sounds like nagging (e.g. 'Why don't you ever call?').
45 They make more direct statements and tend to beat around the bush less often.	**45** They make more indirect statements and tend to beat around the bush more often.
46 They are less verbose and get to the point more quickly.	**46** They tend to be more verbose and don't get to the point very quickly.
47 They say 'uhm-mmm' less often and nod their heads less frequently when listening.	**47** They say 'uhm-mmm' and nod their heads more when listening.

MEN

48 They use 'right' or 'OK' as interjections.

49 They are more silent during conversational lulls.

50 They use fewer intensifiers.

51 They raise fewer topics of conversation.

52 They ignore topics which women raise and usually talk about subjects which they bring up themselves.

53 They use less correct grammar (e.g. 'Who are you goin' with?').

54 They answer questions with a declaration (e.g. Q: 'What's the time?' A: 'It's two o'clock.')

WOMEN

48 They use 'uhm-mmm' as an interjection.

49 They interject 'uhm-mmm' or 'hmmm' during conversational lulls.

50 They use more intensifiers, such as 'few', 'so', 'very', 'really', 'much', 'quite' (e.g. 'It's very pretty', 'It's such a nice day').

51 They raise more topics of conversation.

52 They take up topics which men raise and tend to want to talk about them.

53 They use more correct grammar (e.g. 'With whom are you going?').

54 They answer questions with a question (e.g. Q: 'What's the time?' A: 'It's two o'clock, isn't it?').

MEN	WOMEN
55 They give more command terms (e.g. 'Get me a beer') and do not couch commands with terms of politeness or endearment.	**55** They use fewer command terms and soften them with more tones of politeness and endearment (e.g. 'Darling, would you mind getting me a beer?').
56 They make more declarative statements (e.g. 'It's a nice day').	**56** They make more tentative statements. They use 'tag endings' after making declarative statements, or they use upward inflections which make statements sound like questions (e.g. 'It's a nice day, isn't it?' or 'It's a nice day?').
57 They use fewer psychological or emotional state verbs.	**57** They use more psychological or emotional state verbs, such as 'I feel', 'I love' or 'I hope' (e.g. 'I feel so sad').
58 When answering questions, they offer minimal responses (e.g. 'Yep', 'Yes', 'No', 'Fine'). They use fewer adjectives and descriptive statements.	**58** When answering questions they elaborate more, explain more, using more adjectives and descriptive statements.

MEN	WOMEN
59 They rarely use adjectives of adoration.	**59** They use more adjectives of adoration (e.g. 'adorable', 'charming', 'precious', 'sweet').
60 They use fewer terms of endearment.	**60** They use more terms of endearment (i.e. 'darling', 'dear', 'sweetheart').
61 They use more interjections when changing the topic or when making shifts in conversation (e.g. 'Hey!', 'Oh!', 'By the way!', 'Listen').	**61** They use more conjunctions when changing the topic or when making shifts in conversation (e.g. 'And', 'But', 'However').
62 They use more quantifiers, such as 'always', 'never', 'all' or 'none'.	**62** They use qualifiers, such as 'kind of' or 'a bit'.
63 They ask fewer questions to stimulate conversation.	**63** They ask more questions to stimulate conversation.
64 They rarely discuss their personal life in a business context.	**64** They tend to establish more business relationships through discussing their personal life.

MEN	WOMEN
65 They make more simple requests (e.g. 'I need help with the shopping').	**65** They make more compound requests (e.g. 'Would you be very kind and help me with the shopping?').
66 They use stronger expletives (e.g. 'Damn it!', 'Shit', 'Oh, fuck!', 'I'm pissed off!').	**66** They use milder expressions (e.g. 'Heavens', 'Oh, no!', 'Oh, dear', 'I'm so furious!').
67 They use more slang words and jargon.	**67** They use fewer slang words and jargon.
68 They tend to lecture more often, and to have more of a monologue.	**68** They usually do not lecture, and favour a give-and-take dialogue.

BEHAVIOURAL PATTERN DIFFERENCES

69 They have a more analytical approach to problems.	**69** They have a more emotional approach to problems.
70 They give fewer compliments.	**70** They give more compliments.
71 They are more task-oriented (e.g. they will ask, 'What is everyone going to do?').	**71** They are more maintenance-oriented (e.g. they will ask, 'Is everyone all right?').

MEN	WOMEN
72 They use more teasing and sarcasm to show affection. They are less direct in showing affection.	**72** They use little sarcasm and teasing to show affection. They are more openly direct in showing affection.
73 They appear less intuitive (e.g. 'Am I supposed to be a mind-reader?'). They tend to be less aware of details.	**73** They appear more intuitive and understand more. They tend to be more aware of details.
74 They look at things more critically.	**74** They look at things less critically.
75 They have more difficulty in expressing intimate feelings.	**75** They have less difficulty in expressing intimate feelings.
76 They cry less when frustrated, but shout more.	**76** They cry more when frustrated or hurt.
77 They are more assertive in communication.	**77** They are less assertive in communication.
78 They are likely to impose or force their opinions on others.	**78** They are less likely to impose or force their opinions on others.
79 They swear more.	**79** They swear less.
80 They are more argumentative.	**80** They are less argumentative.

MEN	WOMEN
81 They provide less feedback in conversation.	**81** They provide more feedback in conversation.
82 They laugh and giggle less.	**82** They laugh and giggle more.
83 They tell more anecdotes and jokes.	**83** They tell fewer anecdotes and jokes.
84 They tell more crude and sexually oriented jokes.	**84** They rarely tell sexually oriented or crude jokes.
85 They play more practical jokes and tease by cutting others down (derogatory humour).	**85** They play fewer practical jokes. They appreciate a sense of humour and play on words. Women are less likely to cut others down or exhibit derogatory humour.
86 They are less accusatory	**86** They are more accusatory.
87 They see time as having a beginning, a middle and an end.	**87** They see time as flowing more continuously.
88 They hold fewer grudges.	**88** They hold more grudges.

What Are These Sex Talk Differences?

<table>
<tr><td align="center">MEN</td><td align="center">WOMEN</td></tr>
<tr><td>89 In an argument, they rarely bring up things from the past and mostly stick to the problem at hand.</td><td>89 In an argument, they often bring up things from the past.</td></tr>
<tr><td>90 They talk more about themselves and their accomplishments.</td><td>90 They talk more about other people's accomplishments and minimize their own.</td></tr>
<tr><td>91 They often tease about personal, 'sensitive' issues.</td><td>91 They rarely tease about personal, 'sensitive' issues.</td></tr>
<tr><td>92 They gossip less.</td><td>92 They gossip more.</td></tr>
<tr><td>93 They are more apt to shout and swear to release anger.</td><td>93 They are more apt to cry to release anger.</td></tr>
<tr><td>94 They confront issues and situations less.</td><td>94 They confront issues and situations more.</td></tr>
<tr><td>95 They try to solve problems and troubles.</td><td>95 They try to match troubles by relating similar negative experiences.</td></tr>
<tr><td>96 They are less likely to ask for help. They try to figure things out on their own.</td><td>96 They are more likely to ask for help and accept it.</td></tr>
</table>

MEN	WOMEN
97 They censor their thoughts more. They communicate less through stream of consciousness.	**97** They censor their thoughts less. They communicate more through stream of consciousness.
98 They do not often apologize after a confrontation.	**98** They often apologize after a confrontation.
99 They talk more about what they did, what they are going to do and where they went.	**99** They talk more about how they feel, about what they did and about what they are going to do.
100 They have more difficulty apologizing.	**100** They can apologize more readily and easily.
101 They apologize using less emotion.	**101** They apologize using more emotion.
102 They talk less about relationships with others and family.	**102** They talk more about relationships with others and family.
103 They appear to be less comfortable hearing accolades about themselves and others.	**103** They appear to be more comfortable hearing accolades about themselves and others.
104 They are more blunt.	**104** They are more diplomatic.
105 They tend to take verbal rejection less personally.	**105** They tend to take verbal rejection more personally.

3

The Evolution
of Sex Differences
in Communication

It had only been a few hours since Leanne had given birth to her twins, George and Georgeanne. The two infants were identical except that one was wrapped in a blue blanket, while the other was in a pink blanket and had a tiny pink bow attached to her little tuft of black hair.

That afternoon her husband, George Sr, returned to the hospital to visit his wife and new babies. When he saw George Jr, he immediately picked up the baby and waved his little arm in a 'hello' gesture. He poked George Jr's tummy and started saying he was going to grow up to be a great football player because he had such broad shoulders. George Sr then proceeded to nickname his son his 'little football stud'.

He then went over to his new daughter's cot. He barely touched her. His tone immediately changed. He spoke softly and more gently to her as he lightly touched her chest and cooed, 'You're so beautiful' in a barely audible tone. There was no lively bouncing tone or tummy-poking with little Georgeanne.

At first, Leanne was rather offended that little Georgeanne wasn't greeted with as much enthusiasm as George Jr was. Then she figured that it was not worth making it into a 'major issue'.

NATURE VS. NURTURE

No book on communication could be complete without addressing the topic of why males and females are different. Some reasons are obvious; others are less apparent. Great controversy still surrounds these differences. Are they biological, environmental or a combination of both? Are we different because of the way we are raised or because of our biology, neurochemistry or hormones? For centuries biologists, neurologists, anthropologists, sociologists and psychologists have been searching for a single definitive answer. The only consensus is that a combination of all these variables contributes to differences between the sexes.

Several researchers have discovered that hormones are responsible for 'masculinizing' or 'feminizing' the developing brain in the womb. This allows little boys and little girls to experience the world differently as they mature. This may be why men and women do not handle stress or aggression in the same way. For instance, men may become more physically agitated than women during stressful situations because of an increase in their testosterone level. Women, on the other hand, become more emotional and have more memory loss when there is a lack of the female hormone oestrogen. An increase in oestrogen leads to more water retention, which in turn causes the irritability familiar in premenstrual syndrome (PMS or PMT), according to Beverly Hills gynaecologist and reproductive endocrinologist Dr Gil Mileikowsky.

Other aspects of behaviour are not hormone-related. A woman's ability to nurture, for instance, has not been connected scientifically to oestrogen levels. 'Nurturing' behaviour is mostly a learned phenomenon. After all, adoptive mothers do not have biological hormonal elevations as they have not physically given birth to the child. Yet they usually do a superb job nurturing their infants. Researcher Harry Harlow's experiments with female monkeys at the University of Wisconsin also confirm that nurturing is a form of learned behaviour instead of something that is hormonally influenced. He found that female monkeys raised in isolation were not very effective at nurturing their young, despite the fact that their hormone level was naturally increased at the time of giving birth.

In essence, hormones do seem to have some influence on the behaviour of the sexes. But it is not this alone which affects male and female behaviour patterns.

ARE SEX DIFFERENCES RELATED TO BRAIN DEVELOPMENT?

Yes! Studies confirm that male and female brains develop at different rates, which does create some differences between the sexes.

When Joyce, a thirty-three-year-old mother of four, came to see me, she was deeply concerned about her young son Bobby's speaking ability. 'I think Bobby has a problem with his speech,' she said. 'In no way does he measure up to the way my three girls spoke when they were his age. He's much slower. That's why I think there's something wrong with him.'

After doing a complete and comprehensive speech and language evaluation on Bobby, I found he was within normal limits for speech and language development at his age. His mother was relieved when I assured her that there was nothing wrong with him and that most boys develop these skills slightly more slowly than girls. So I told her it was not valid to compare Bobby's speech and language development with that of his three older sisters.

Research shows that the left side of girls' brains develops more rapidly than that of boys, and this causes increased development in verbal functioning. This may be why little girls learn to talk sooner than little boys, have a better vocabulary and pronunciation, read earlier, excel in memory at a younger age, and can learn foreign languages more rapidly than boys do at the same age. On the other hand, boys develop the right side of their brain faster than girls do. As a result they have earlier visual-spatial, logical and perceptual development. For this reason they tend to be better at mathematics, problem solving, building and figuring out puzzles than girls.

In addition, several studies have shown that, as infant girls develop, they are more interested in toys with faces than infant boys are. Infant girls prefer to play with stuffed animals and dolls, while infant boys are drawn to blocks or anything that can be manipulated.

It must be pointed out, however, that these brain differences only exist in children; eventually boys and girls catch up with one another. The brain function balances out during school years, as Dr David Shucard, a researcher at the National Jewish Hospital National Asthma Center in Denver, discovered. His study found that boy and girl babies definitely use different sides of the brain when listening to music and fairy tales, which he measured through electrical sensors and recorded on graph paper. However, he noted that these apparent differences disappeared as the brain matured. Some studies, however, show that men may still retain a greater capacity to utilize the right side of their brain, while women may use the left side of their brain to a large extent.

Neurologist Dr Roger Gorski of UCLA confirms that there are structural differences between men and women's brains. There are also sex differences in the nuclei and in the circuitry of the brain which may account for men and women doing things similarly but using different parts of the brain when doing them. This has been proved by brain researchers Cecile Naylor at the Bowman Gray School of Medicine in North Carolina, Dutch neuroscientist Dick Swaaband, UCLA's neuroscientist Roger Gorski, and Christine de la Coste of Stanford University in California.

In male and female stroke victims, even when the damage to the brain is in the left hemisphere, which controls speech and language functioning, women are more likely to experience greater recovery of their speaking skills than men are. Dr Gorski explains that the reason for this may be that female brains are less lateralized, meaning that women tend to use both the right and left hemispheres for speech whereas men tend to use only the left. In other words, women utilize other parts of their brain to aid their recovery.

While scientists continue to argue that men and women think and act differently from one another because of biological differences, there are those who believe that men and women do so because of the way they have been brought up – because of their environment. Perhaps these minimal brain function differences, evident from birth through childhood, are reinforced by the child's environment. Perhaps these differences are reinforced by parents themselves. Let's explore these possibilities further.

OUR ENVIRONMENT – HOW WE TREAT OUR BOY AND GIRL INFANTS

One of the most telling of all examples concerning how a child is raised and conditioned by its parents was Leanne's experience of the way her husband reacted to their male and female newborn twins. But his behaviour was not all that uncommon, as studies have shown. One of the most poignant and classic examples was conducted at Harvard University.

Both men and women were put into a room with infant boys and girls. In almost every case, both genders spoke 'louder' to the boys than they did to the girls. Their voices were softer and they made more cooing sounds to the little girls. They even spoke different words to them. Comments such as 'You are so sweet', 'Look at the little dolls', 'You're so pretty' and 'You're a little sweetheart' were verbalized to the girls and not to the boys. On the other hand, the boys were handled more physically and robustly. They were picked up, bounced around and tickled more than the girls. The girls were stroked and caressed more. The boys were told things like 'Hey, you little pumpkin head' or 'Hey, big guy.'

In another study, which revealed how differently male and female infants are socialized, psychiatrist Michael Lewis showed that mothers repeatedly looked at and talked to their infant girls more often than they did their infant boys. This was so until the child was two years of age.

Psychologist Carol Z. Malatesta, associate professor of psychology at Long Island University in New York, videotaped facial expressions of mothers and their infants during play. She observed that mothers showed a wider range of emotional responses to the girls than to the boys.

However, when the girls showed anger their mothers showed greater facial disapproval than they did when the boys showed anger. She suggests that the mothers' responses to their children might be the reason why baby girls grow up smiling more, are more sociable, and are better able to 'read' or detect a person's emotions than boys.

While reading up on research in this area, I discovered that a child's sex role expectations and parental expectations often elicit a response even before the child is born. Our preconceived notions of how we will treat our little boy or little girl are clearly illustrated in Billy Bigalow's fantasy about his unborn child in the musical *Carousel*. Remember how he sings about 'My Boy Bill'? His voice is energetic, loud and forceful. His pace is fast, as he sings about all the things he and his 'imagined son', Bill, would do together. Suddenly we hear Billy Bigalow's tone change to a delicate, soft, tender one as he concludes that this unborn child could turn out to be a girl.

It is no wonder that parents' stereotyped impressions play such an integral role in the way they socialize their children. Nursery rhymes, cartoons and books also help to perpetuate these stereotypes. Remember the nursery rhyme:

> *There was a little girl who had a little curl*
> *Right in the middle of her forehead.*
> *And when she was good*
> *She was very very good.*
> *But when she was bad she was horrid.*

Well, what exactly did this little girl do that was so 'horrid'? Did she squeal or jump up and down or have a mind of her own? Did she push or shove someone? If this fictitious child was a 'little boy' instead of a 'little girl', would we call 'him' horrid? Would we accept it if 'his' behaviour was more 'aggressive' than our imaginary 'little girl's' behaviour?

Without realizing what they are doing, parents recite these nursery rhymes and so they are mindlessly passed down from one generation to the next. They perpetuate the stereotypes of how we expect our little girls and little boys to act. This is evident not only in the majority of our nursery rhymes but also in cartoons. In fact, psychologist Susan B. Kaiser at the University of California at Davis has found that, too often, female characters perpetuated blatant stereotypes such as 'the damsel in distress', 'the frumpy housewife', 'the helpless senior citizen', 'the sexy heroine' and 'the swooning cheerleader'.

Children's books are another area where stereotypic sex differences are apparent. Even though current research shows that great progress has already been made in children's books, even greater strides can be made if all stereotype male and female portrayals are eliminated.

SEX DIFFERENCE EXPECTATIONS – GROWING OLDER

As children grow older their parents still tend to socialize them differently, as Jean Berko Gleason and Esther Blank Greifs' illustrative study points out. In their book *Men's Speech to Young Children in Language Gender Society* these researchers examined how men talked to young children. They found that fathers used more 'command' terms than mothers; also, the men gave more commands to their sons than to their daughters. This study may show why little boys use more command terms themselves and are not as polite as little girls during play activity. Boys will often use phrases like 'Gimme that' or 'Go away', whereas little girls will often say, 'Please give that to me' or 'Please stop bothering me.'

On the other hand, little girls' speech and language patterns differ from boys' because they too have been raised differently. In fact, girls have been found to incorporate many 'female' traits in their speech communication patterns from as early as four years of age. A linguist's recent observation of thirty-five nursery school children found that 'female' speech patterns emerged on a consistent basis. The little girls were found to use 'tag endings' (such as 'She has a pretty dress, doesn't she?'). They were also found to use more 'terms of endearment' when playing with their dolls.

As children grow older, their parents continue to treat them differently based on sex. They will tolerate certain kinds of behaviour from boys that they would never tolerate from girls, and vice versa. In essence, little boys are given different messages concerning what is acceptable from those that little girls are given. Two-year-old Shauna was reprimanded for hitting and biting and told why her behaviour was unacceptable, whereas two-year-old Sean would also be stopped and reprimanded, but would not be told that his behaviour was unacceptable.

Susanna was a forty-year-old, very progressive and socially aware mother of a robust, precocious, lively six-year-old girl. Her daughter's school reports kept saying that Jennifer was 'too loud' or 'too talkative', or 'Jennifer is always screaming in the playground', or 'Jennifer cannot sit still' and so on. Finally, Susanna decided to have a talk with Jennifer's teacher concerning her daughter's so-called 'behavioural problems' at school. But before she even sat down the teacher blurted out in a hostile tone, 'Jennifer is a terror! She yells and screams and won't stop talking. Little girls aren't supposed to act like that. She acts like a bad little boy.'

Even though Susanna was not pleased that her daughter was disrupting the class, she was not particularly worried.

She shrugged off her daughter's exhibition of 'male' behaviour as 'tomboy' antics. But had the situation been reversed – had Susanna had a son who exhibited 'female' behaviour – his being labelled a 'sissy', a pejorative term, would probably have upset her. In essence, if a girl does not conform to stereotype she is still accepted by her peers at this age. However, with a boy, his peers – or society, for that matter – may not be as tolerant. A shy boy who is extremely sensitive and cries, who would rather play with the girls than the other boys, can have his life turned into a living nightmare by his peers.

WHAT BOYS AND GIRLS TALK ABOUT

Throughout the socialization period little boys not only play differently but talk about different things from little girls. Early in life little girls tend to talk about people – who is upset by whom, and who likes whom. They will usually talk about friends. Since most little girls tend to play together in pairs or small groups, they will usually tell one another 'secrets' in order to bond their friendship. These 'secrets' are usually about people. Studies also show that girls between eight and twelve speak more about school, their wishes and their needs.

On the other hand, little boys at that age will talk about things and 'activities'. Little boys are usually socialized in groups and mostly talk about their activities – what they all are doing, and who's the 'best' at any particular activity.

Observations indicate that, as teenagers, girls seem to talk mostly about boys, clothes and their weight, while teenage boys talk about sports and the mechanics or functions of things. A New York-based youth market consulting and research firm, Xtreme Inc., found results which parallel this finding. In their recent survey of close to two thousand teenagers from twelve to eighteen it was discovered that the biggest event for girls was to have a boyfriend and 'make out'. It was also shown that, even though boys were equally interested in sex, they were also just as interested in cars and sports.

These differences are often carried over through puberty into adulthood, at which time the content of women's talk usually centres around people and relationships, diet, clothing and physical appearance. On the other hand, according to a survey by psychologist Dr Adelaide Haas of the State University of New York, adult males usually talk about activities such as sports or what was done at work, cars, news, music or the mechanics of things.

A similar study by sociolinguist Dr Cheris Kramarae of the University of Illinois further illustrates this point. She found that 'male speech' was characterized by both sexes as being more forceful, dominating, boastful, blunt, authoritarian and to the point than 'female speech', which she found to be perceived as friendlier, gentler, faster, more emotional and more enthusiastic, tending to focus on more 'trivial' topics than men's speech did.

With such vast differences not only in how they talk but what they talk about, it stands to reason why, when they become adults, men and women have such a difficult time talking to one another.

4

Improving Your Personal and Social Relationships with the Opposite Sex

This chapter will explore how the SEX TALK DIF-FERENCES listed in Chapter 2 affect our personal relationships with the opposite sex. First, we will look at male–female attraction and see what appeals to the opposite sex. Then we will explore how men and women fail to communicate on a personal level and consider what can be done to improve the situation.

Based on the 105 differences in Chapter 2, there appear to be twenty SEX TALK DIFFERENCES which apply to your personal life. If not understood, they can have a harmful affect on your personal relationships.

SEX TALK DIFFERENCES

1 Men and women have different body language. Men have more inattentive, sloppy body language than women.

2 Men and women have different head postures. Women tend to bow their heads down while speaking, whereas men tend to tilt their heads at an angle when listening and speaking.

3 Men and women gesture differently, which can be misinterpreted by one another. When conversing, men tend to gesture away from the body, giving women the impression of not being as sensitive.

4 Men and women differ when it comes to taking up space in a room. Men take up more space and also invade personal space more often than women.

5 Men tend to avoid eye contact more often than women, especially in positive situations.

6 Men do not provide as much facial response as women. Men smile less and frown and squint more when listening.

7 Men and women have different tones and vocal animation. Men tend to have a more nasal and less enthusiastic voice.

8 Men tend to interrupt more than women, do not give as much immediate verbal feedback such as 'uhm-mmm', and use minimal responses. During conversation, men also tend to change the subject more often if a woman has brought it up than if they have brought it up themselves.

9 Men and women differ in the amount of details they use when describing something.

10 Men tend to engage in more monologue than dialogue; with women it is the opposite.

11   Women tend to have better listening skills than men, as they provide greater visual and verbal feedback.

12   Men and women differ in the way in which they give compliments to one another.

13   Men and women let off steam or anger differently. Men tend to shout, while women tend to cry more.

14   Men and women accuse and blame each other differently. Women tend to be more accusatory, yet indirect in their accusations. They will usually say, 'How come you never call me,' while men will say directly, 'You didn't call.'

15   Men and women differ in terms of asking for help. Men will usually try to figure things out on their own, whereas women will readily ask for help.

16   Men express their requests with commands, whereas women express theirs with terms of endearment ('Get me a beer' versus 'Darling, would you mind getting me a beer?').

17   Men and women joke differently, as men's humour tends to be more crude and sexually oriented. They also play more practical jokes.

18   Men and women talk about different things. Women tend to talk about self-improvement, clothes, other people and relationships, while men tend to talk about sports, business, mechanical things, cars and music.

19   Men and women take verbal rejection, such as being told 'No', differently. More women than men tend to personalize rejection.

20 Men and women differ in disclosing information about themselves. Men tend to disclose less personal information, while women tend to disclose more.

Given these twenty SEX TALK DIFFERENCES, it is no wonder that men and women have difficulty communicating with one another on a personal level. In fact, the following alleged conversation between the Prince and Princess of Wales seems symbolic of the communication gap between the sexes.

THE COMMUNICATION GAP HITS THE ROYAL COUPLE

I have been collecting information about sex differences in communication for the past seventeen years. About ten years ago I came across an article in the 18 May 1981 edition of *Newsweek* magazine. It discussed a tape-recorded, long-distance telephone conversation between Prince Charles and the then Lady Diana Spencer, which occurred while they were courting. Transcripts of the audiotapes, made by a person who eavesdropped on their conversation, were printed in the magazine.

Diana Won't it be nice when we can go out together again?

Charles Perhaps we won't know what to talk about.

Diana Well, you can start by telling me about all those blondes who chase you and I can laugh because you belong to me.

Charles Yes.

Diana But probably you will talk about nothing but polo.

After this glimpse into Charles and Diana's 'small talk' prior to their wedding, it comes as no surprise that their marriage is now in trouble according to the press.

This conversation is a clear example of a couple not speaking each other's language. Charles appears to ignore Diana's request. He does not respond to her question, 'Won't it be nice when we can go out together again?' He does not respond with terms of endearment or warmth such as, 'Yes, sweetheart, it would be. I can't wait to see you either.' Instead, he uses sarcasm as humour, as demonstrated by his comment, 'Perhaps we won't know what to talk about.' It is in this comment that we see the signs of disparity in their relationship – they seem not to have much in common, and so they have little to talk about.

She, in turn, responds with, 'Well, you can start by telling me about all those blondes who chase you and I can laugh because you belong to me.' This response is indicative of Diana wanting more reassurance concerning their relationship. It is also her attempt to establish more intimacy and more security between them.

Charles's reply is merely, 'Yes'. What does Charles mean by his single word response? By not reassuring her, he leaves Diana feeling insecure about the relationship. By his lack of communication, he is avoiding intimacy. In order to save face and recover from Charles's seemingly cold response Diana attempts to regain her self-esteem by her comment, 'But probably you will talk about nothing but polo.' This clearly reflects her frustration with Charles's not 'opening up'. Her statement also shows her frustration and realization that they have little to communicate about, even at such an early stage of their relationship.

Here is a further excerpt from Charles and Diana's alleged conversation indicating Charles's premonition that their relationship would not work out:

Charles   I'm glad to be out of New Zealand. Now I know everything I need to know about the paper in-

	dustry in New Zealand. But I ask myself all the time about what you were up to.
Diana	I really miss you, darling. I'm not really alone, but it bothers me that thousands of people can be with you and I can't. I'm really jealous.
Charles	Yes, I know. It's too bad, but in a couple of years you might be glad to get rid of me for a while.
Diana	Never.
Charles	I'll remind you of that in ten years' time.

Certainly, if any man communicates to a woman in that way he is headed for a rude awakening, as this is a total turn-off to most women.

Charles neglected to respond to Diana's emotions. For example, in response to her statement, 'I really miss you, darling,' Charles merely replies, 'Yes, I know.' This makes him sound rather selfish and egotistical. Instead of saying something endearing back to Diana such as, 'I miss you too, sweetheart,' he says, 'Yes I know . . . in a couple of years you might be glad to get rid of me for a while.' This statement further distances him from Diana. Even though the comment may have been made in jest, in actuality it makes Diana feel alienated as indicated by her optimistic, romantically enthusiastic, fairy-tale-like response – 'Never' – as she attempts to reassert her position as the one and only woman in his life forever. Charles continues with what he may perceive as another humorous quip, 'I'll remind you of that in ten years' time', which further sets him apart from Diana.

Prince Charles is definitely not alone. Millions of men do not know how to talk to women. As a result, ultimately – and unknowingly – they wind up alienating those they care about most.

WHAT DO WE TALK ABOUT?

Many men and women experience difficulty in having fulfilling conversations, as revealed in the one between Charles and Diana. In essence, men and women really do not know what to say to one another. A lovely thirty-year-old Canadian news reporter told me that she had broken up with her boyfriend whom she had been dating for a year. When I asked her what had happened, she answered, 'He was just too boring. He was a sports reporter, and all he ever talked about was sport and his Corvette. He never wanted to talk about things which I found interesting.'

The differences between what men and women talk about were extremely interesting to one of my clients, Edward. He attended his first 'shower' party for a girl who was having a baby, and had the honour of being the only male in a roomful of women. Edward learned who was having an affair, who was getting divorced and who was now available. He heard about labour pains, period pains and detailed accounts of various 'female-related' operations. He even learned that one woman's pubic-hair had never grown back after her hysterectomy. He discovered which men were 'great in bed and why', and how to give yourself a facial that only takes five minutes.

Edward told me it was the greatest party he had ever attended. It made him feel so 'open' and so 'human', and he felt privileged to be allowed in on such intimate conversations. This whole experience gave him a better appreciation of women and a greater sensitivity to how they feel and think.

Men must learn what women enjoy talking about. In a recent study by Dr Adelaide Haas of the Department of Speech Communication at the State University of New York, she found that the most common topics discussed by females were:

1. men
2. food
3. relationship or family problems, and
4. clothes.

Other topics that women talked about were news events and work-related issues. Women like to discuss feelings, as well as more socially oriented matters. On the other hand, Dr Haas found that men talked more about:

1. women
2. news events
3. sports
4. arts, and
5. sex.

In order to have a meaningful conversation with the opposite sex, one must become aware of this difference in likes and dislikes. It is essential for women to be more willing to talk about activities and related issues, as men do. If you don't know anything about these topics, learn about them. Just watch the news and read the sports pages.

On the other hand, if men want to have better conversations with women they need to pay more attention to interpersonal relationships, other people, situations and self-improvement. If both sexes made equal efforts to learn what the other sex wants to talk about, that would certainly help bridge the conversational gap between men and women.

WHAT APPEALS TO THE OPPOSITE SEX?

Just as important as *what* is said is *how* it is said. In fact, how we say things can determine whether or not a person of the opposite sex will be attracted to us.

Men's body language differs from women's mainly in sitting and head posture but also in other ways. Women tend to gesture closer to their bodies, whereas men gesture away from their bodies. This gives men a more authoritative air. If you take up more space and gesture outwards, it gives others the visual impression that you are definite and adamant about your statements. In a personal situation, this may not be the impression men would want to project. Instead, less aggressive gestures – made towards the body – as well as being more conscious of the amount of space and room that the man takes up, would give the woman the impression that he is being more sensitive, caring and receptive.

Fidgeting and rocking back and forth are also quite common in men but not in women. Doing this while talking to a woman gives her the impression that you don't care, are not interested, or are in a hurry and need to leave. Besides being very distracting, it also alienates the woman.

APPEALING EYE AND FACE CONTACT

One of the major hurdles on the way to better communication is better eye and face contact. If you do not appear to be interested or listening, there will definitely be no communication. And without positive communication, which includes looking into the other person's face and eyes, even if you sense physical attraction it will not be encouraged.

In order to become more attractive to the opposite sex you need to maintain good eye and facial contact. You need to look directly at the person when you speak to them. You need to smile, look at the person and not shy away. Look at the person's eyes for a few moments, then look at their nose, their mouth, their chin and then their entire face. All this should take just a few seconds. Then repeat the process. By doing this, you will appear to be genuinely listening to the other person. Your interest will show.

For instance, Jeremy was very attracted to Susan whom he met at a party. Yet he panicked and became shy when he realized he was interested in her. During their conversation, instead of looking directly at her he looked down and off to the side, which made him appear as if he was definitely *not* interested in her. When Jeremy did manage to look at her, his head was cocked at an angle which gave the impression he didn't really care about her.

On top of that, Jeremy appeared to be paying more attention to Susan's breasts than he did to her face. In reality he wasn't even thinking about her breasts. Yet he was so uncomfortable and had such poor eye contact that he just zeroed in on them. This was a total turn-off to Susan, who quickly ended their acquaintance and walked away.

Lack of eye contact is a typically male trait that can be changed. Men should learn to look into a woman's eyes – what happened to Jeremy should not happen to you. You need to maintain eye and face contact consistently to give the impression that you are really interested in the woman. Yet communication should also go beyond the face and eyes – the voice and body convey rejection or acceptance as well.

PRESENTING AN APPEALING VOICE

In my own research I found that the way a person spoke was even more important than the way that person looked.

It didn't matter whether they had a physical deformity or were facially unattractive. If they had good speaking skills, they had a better lot in life.

What maintains a person's interest is the way you communicate with them. It is not only your body language, your gestures and your facial language but the tone which you use that makes a person want to get to know you.

There are plenty of screen actors with physical flaws who become exciting and appealing when we watch them move and when we see and hear them talk. It is called 'chemistry' or, in Hollywood, 'screen presence'. Actors with natural good looks, like Sean Connery, Mel Gibson, Michael Douglas, Kathleen Turner or Kim Basinger, become even more sexy, exciting and appealing when we watch their body language, gestures and facial language and then listen to the tones that come out of them. These are all things which you can change and learn to adapt in order to attract and become more attractive to the opposite sex.

A tone can turn a person on or off and a person's voice is certainly a barometer of how they are feeling. As I have constantly said in my lectures and books, what goes on in a person's head and in their heart will usually come across in their voice. A person can tell if another is in a good mood or a bad one just by the way they say 'Hello'. All your emotions – anger, love, sadness, dishonesty or fear – are reflected in the way you sound, so it is important to have a good voice especially when communicating with the opposite sex.

Ilona is a beautiful forty-five-year-old woman married to a well-known businessman. She dresses like a countess, has a regal posture and a great deal of 'presence'. However, when she speaks her voice is nasal and has a very harsh and alienating quality. She also talks loudly and much too fast. Although she is constantly invited to parties with her husband, very few people talk to her. The vocal image she projects is inconsistent with her physical image.

I taught Ilona how to speak in a more flowing, modulating tone. I taught her how to slow down her speech by drawing out her vowel tones, how to open her jaw in order to create less nasality, and how to modulate her volume level. When she had mastered all this she discovered a whole new world of friends. Changing her vocal tones literally changed her life for the better.

The tone of your voice is essential for attracting the opposite sex. If your voice is monotonous or loud, or its tone is too high-pitched or otherwise annoying, people, especially the opposite sex, will often reject you. For my book *Talk To Win* I conducted a Gallup Poll aimed at discovering the speech habits that annoyed people most. The answer was those who talk too softly, too loudly or too quickly, who have a monotonous tone, who use filler words such as 'um' and 'you know', who have a nasal whine, use poor grammar, have a high-pitched voice, interrupt others and use swear words. If you are guilty of any of these habits, eliminate them from your life once and for all if you want to appeal to the opposite sex.

TO ATTRACT, YOU NEED
TO BE HEARD

When a person feels shy or uncomfortable with the opposite sex, it is not uncommon for them to look away and for their voice to drop off when they speak. This is definitely not the best way to attract someone. If they can't hear you, they may feel that what you have to say is not very important.

This happened to a client of mine, Jason, an extremely shy twenty-five-year-old who came to me for help in getting over his shyness and also to improve his vocal quality. One day he told me that he had met a woman whom he really liked but did not know what to say to her. He said that when he was talking to her she kept saying, 'Sorry, I didn't hear you.' He knew that his tone dropped off, but thought there was nothing he could do about it. He felt dumb and stupid, as he put it, and was embarrassed about the image he was projecting to her.

Jason's feelings are not that unusual. He has such low self-esteem that he does not feel he is important enough to be heard. In addition, he is so busy being self-conscious about how he is coming across to the woman that he loses sight of his intention, which is to show his interest in her. If you can relate to Jason's experience, keep in mind that when you meet a member of the opposite sex, being 'interested' in them is more important than appearing 'interesting' and entertaining yourself. Asking questions will help you feel more secure: it will allow you to communicate and so help project who you really are.

AN ENTHUSIASTIC VOICE

One of my clients, Patricia, was fixed up for a blind date with what her best girlfriend described as her 'ideal' man. He certainly appeared to have all the attributes she wanted: a good job, athletic ability, a great sense of fashion and financial stability; he also came from a good family. However, when she met him her opinion changed radically. After talking to him for just one minute she regretted ever opening the door. He was such a monotonous bore, sounding empty and hollow. Patricia couldn't wait for the date to be over. So although her date was basically an interesting character, she wouldn't even give him a second chance. His speech habits were so annoying that she was no longer attracted to him.

Enthusiasm is one of the most important ways to attract a person. If you want to be more appealing, don't be afraid to show your enthusiasm. Say, for instance, 'I'm thrilled to meet you' or 'I've heard so many wonderful things about you.' Have some bounce in your tone, and let your excitement about meeting the new person show in your voice. In this way you can be more certain that your interaction will start on a positive note.

FAILURE TO COMMUNICATE, AND HOW TO IMPROVE IT

The next section deals with the various ways in which men and women fail to get through to one another, based on the SEX TALK DIFFERENCES in communication, and then with the various ways of improving the situation. You will learn about the other person and how to avoid annoying communication patterns which may be misinterpreted. These include changing the subject and interrupting, which are very male, sex-biased traits. You will also learn how to be a better listener, which can help you avoid unnecessary arguments. You will learn how to say things in a manner that won't be offensive to your mate, and to say what you really want and mean without causing offence. Finally you will learn how to be more emotionally expressive.

PUTTING OUT
THE WRONG MESSAGE

There are many ways in which men show their inability to communicate with women. One of the most obvious is the frequency with which their verbal and non-verbal actions send out messages that conflict with their true feelings. Here is a typical example.

Carl is an extraordinarily handsome, well-built, thirty-eight-year-old lawyer who hates going to parties or social activities. Even though he seems to have it all – a nice home, a smart car and financial security – he doesn't seem to have any 'luck' with women, as he puts it. After much coercion by Michael, a colleague at his law firm, Carl relented and attended Michael's party after being assured that a lot of attractive single women would be there. Even though he felt uncomfortable, he was glad he had accepted the invitation as he noticed across the room a woman to whom he was immediately drawn.

He observed that she was vivacious and seemed to talk to everyone around her. She had a big radiant smile and appeared open and warm. Carl immediately went over to her and said, 'Hi, I've been noticing you from across the room, and you have a gorgeous smile.' The woman beamed and thanked him. He then noticed that she kept smiling and looking at him, which suddenly made him feel uncomfortable and self-conscious. Even though he started feeling awkward, he forced himself to shake hands with her and introduced himself. 'I'm Carl Templer,' he said, as his eyes shifted downwards, reaching out his hand. He still kept looking downward until the woman introduced herself as Jennifer Dalton. Then his eyes began darting everywhere. Since they were standing near a sofa, Carl said, 'Sit down. Let's talk.' The woman agreed, and continued smiling at Carl. When they were seated, Carl seemed to be taking up the entire sofa: his arms were spread out around the back, his legs jutted out in front, and he had adopted a semi-reclining position.

As he talked about himself and what he did for a living, he kept fidgeting and moving around. This made him appear uncomfortable. His gestures were broad and sweeping when he spoke, which made him seem overbearing. As he continued to talk to Jennifer, he hardly looked at her. Instead, he kept looking off to the side – which made him appear as though he was more interested in the other people at the party. He hardly looked at Jennifer's face when he talked to her, and whenever he did manage to look at her his eyes moved down and seemed to lock in on her breasts. When she asked him a question, he ignored it and kept on talking about himself and other subjects. Jennifer began to feel as though Carl was having a one-way conversation – with himself. Her presence didn't seem to matter. Eventually, she decided she had had enough.

She strained a phoney smile, got up and said that she would be right back. While making her way to the other side of the room she ran into her girlfriend, Cathy, with whom she had come to the party. This was their conversation:

Cathy	Wow! You lucked out! Who was that gorgeous hunk you were talking to?'
Jennifer	Gorgeous hunk? Asshole is more like it!
Cathy	Are you serious? What did he do?
Jennifer	First of all the jerk orders me to sit down like a dog and then he kept talking to my boobs the whole time – not even looking up at me. Then, when he did manage to break away from them, he'd look to see who else was coming in the room. He had a cocky air about him and acted like he was so great. It was like he was looking down at me and judging me. What a snot! Then, all he

kept talking about was himself, his stupid cases and his stupid car. Ugh! Forget it!

Cathy   Oh, no! What a geek! And to think I thought he was cute!

After realizing that Jennifer was not going to come back, Carl went to find Michael. When he found him, this was their conversation.

Michael   (all smiles, patting Carl on the back) See, I told you you'd meet some nice-looking babes here. Aren't you glad you came?

Carl   No, not really! That chick I was talking to . . . .

Michael   Yeah. Boy, did she have a nice pair!

Carl   I guess. But what a bitch! Here I was being my nice-guy self, telling her all about what I do – and then she splits, like she couldn't care less. She probably figured out that I wasn't a partner yet and wasn't a millionaire. I probably didn't have enough money for her.

Michael   Don't lose any sleep over *her*. It's good you found out now. You wouldn't have wanted her anyway!

Neither Carl nor Jennifer had a clue about what was really happening. They completely misread and misinterpreted each other's signals because they didn't understand the SEX TALK DIFFERENCES between men and women. Had they understood, they would probably have enjoyed the evening together and might even have begun to date one another. After all, the chemistry was certainly there at first sight.

Here's what went wrong. Carl gave off the wrong messages. Basically, he's a nice guy; he wants desperately to meet a woman and have a relationship with her, but unfortunately he doesn't know how to go about it. His first mistake was giving Jennifer an order: 'Sit down. Let's talk.' Instead of using a command he needed to ask a question, which would have made him sound more polite – 'Why don't we both sit down here so we can talk?'

In addition, he will never interest a woman without maintaining facial contact. Even though Carl is uncomfortable, he needs to force himself to take a breath in, hold it and then let it out so he can get more control over his body language and over what he is saying. He needs to maintain facial contact and look at the entire face of the woman he is talking to. Looking off to the side made him appear as though he wasn't really interested in Jennifer. Instead, he needs to rotate looking at 'parts of her face' – her eyes, her nose and her mouth – and then at her 'whole face' – not at her breasts. If he does happen to glance at her breasts, under no circumstances should he keep his eyes glued there. Even though he may be feeling nervous and uncomfortable, his looking down will be interpreted as lack of interest and extreme rudeness. In reality Carl wasn't even thinking about Jennifer's breasts, but because he was so uncomfortable and had such poor eye contact he just zeroed in on her chest. Inevitably that was a total turn-off to Jennifer.

Carl also needs to take a look at his posture – he should position his buttocks back in the chair or sofa first, and then sit up so his back is straight up against the chair. He also needs to be conscious of how much room and space he is taking up, so that he doesn't overpower and overwhelm the woman. Even though it is a typically male body posture, a sloppy, reclined sitting position with his head cocked to one side gives the impression that he is snobbish, judgemental and aloof.

Next, he needs to find something else to talk about besides himself and how great he is. He needs to ask the woman questions about her life and respond to her answers. He needs to have a dialogue with her – not a monologue with himself. When a woman brings up a question or topic, he needs to deal with that issue and not change the subject. He needs to ask another question that is related to the one which she asked, so that they can continue their dialogue. In this way he can learn more about her, and she in turn can learn more about him.

DIALOGUE NOT MONOLOGUE – FIND OUT ABOUT THE OTHER PERSON

Often when a man and woman first meet they are nervous and want the other person to know everything about them as quickly as possible. But getting to know a person takes time. You cannot do it all in one day, one evening or one hour. So in order to learn more about each other, men and women need to ask one another more open-ended questions, such as, 'What do you think of the situation in the Middle East?' as opposed to 'Do you like what is happening in the Middle East?' Since men have been found to answer questions with one-word responses more often than women, it is in a woman's best interest to ask these open-ended questions in order to elicit a more verbal response from the man. Instead of asking a question that requires a 'Yes' or 'No' answer, create an opportunity for more dialogue to develop.

'Dialogue' is the key word here. Since men have a tendency to engage in a monologue, it is essential for them to keep this tendency in mind and attempt to curb it when speaking to women. Remember, getting to know a person of the opposite sex is a give-and-take proposition. Tell them a little bit about yourself, then ask them about themselves. Hopefully, they will do the same. If they do, you are off to a great start in bridging the communication gap with the opposite sex.

BRIDGING THE SEX GAP THROUGH LOOKING AND LISTENING

Another way in which men and women communicate differently is in the area of listening – women exhibit better listening skills. In general, both male and female public speakers look more to the women in the audience than to the men. This is because women tend to give more non-verbal cues which express agreement. They smile more, nod with approval and say 'uhm-mmm' to a greater extent than men. The implications are that women tend to be positive listeners. Men need to become better listeners, which in turn can help them enhance their relationships with women. Women can help them here, and in so doing eliminate many potential arguments as well as create closer bonds between the sexes.

Even though it has been said that women tend to be more intuitive than men, this is a myth. Perhaps this misconception is due to women's attention to detail as well as their sensitivity to body language and cues. But men can become more intuitive and have better social relationships with women if they learn to be more observant. They need to provide women with more auditory feedback cues, such as 'uhm-mmm', and more visual feedback cues, such as head nods. Using more positive non-verbal cues will give the impression that the man is interested in the conversation.

Since women are so much more conditioned to give feedback, they tend to feel more at ease with a man when he does this too. This, in turn, provides the woman with more feedback. Good eye contact and nodding ensure that the talker knows that the listener understands what is being said. And while listening, it is important for men not

59

to fidget, tap their foot or fiddle with objects, as this can be very disconcerting to the woman.

Next, the man needs to pay attention to the ideas that the woman is conveying and not necessarily to the facts. Men frequently interrupt to pick on details and correct the woman; this is unacceptable. Instead, listen to the entire statement. Men need to watch themselves for jumping to conclusions or finishing sentences for women. Unfortunately this happens all too often, especially in couples who have been together for a long time. Men must learn to lean forward and pay closer attention to conversation. They must try to stay more focused and concentrate on what the woman is saying. They need to observe how a woman is communicating – not only what she is saying, but how she is saying it. Men must pay attention to a woman's intonation and her emotions, which will allow them to gain more information about the woman and in essence learn more about her.

Women's number one gripe about having conversations with men is their interruptions; a Gallup Poll I commissioned in 1987 confirmed this. In order to help control their impulses to interrupt, men should use the following technique. Before you interrupt, suck in a breath of air through your mouth for three seconds, then hold it for three seconds, and finally exhale it for six seconds. This technique will help you gain more control over both what you want to say and how you say it.

Another form of interruption for which men are notorious is changing the subject, in particular if it was a woman who brought up the topic in the first place. If you are a woman and notice that the man is changing the subject too often, speak up. Only then will you be heard. If you get annoyed by this, say, 'Let's get back to what we were talking about,' or 'I don't want to change the subject yet', and then return to the original topic of conversation.

Women need to assert themselves, take charge and not let themselves be bulldozed or intimidated by certain types of male communication behaviour – which can be rude at times. Women also need to point out any form of behaviour which annoys them; this will stop them harbouring any hard feelings towards the man, which could give the wrong impression.

Candy, a client of mine, asked me what she should do about her boyfriend, who constantly interrupted her and hardly ever let her finish what she was trying to say. As a result she always lost her train of thought in conversation with him, which frustrated and angered her so much that she would sulk and refuse to speak to him any more. I told Candy to fight fire with fire and interrupt him back. She should not let him finish his statements unless she was allowed to finish hers. Instead, she needed to say, 'Please let me finish', and continue her conversation without getting intimidated.

You do not have to be rude to stop someone from constantly changing the topic. Just smile and say politely, 'Excuse me, please let me finish.' This will usually convey the message; often people may not even be aware of what they are doing unless you tell them. On the other hand, if you do want to change the subject, let the other person know what you are doing so they can follow your lead. You need to say, 'I'd like to change the topic at this point and talk about such and such.' By doing this you won't appear rude, and you can still discuss what you wish. Just let the person know where you are leading the conversation. But don't do it too often, and be careful about appearing too controlling, selfish and rude. Being aware of this can help you to close the communication gap with the opposite sex even further.

DON'T BE STINGY
WITH YOUR COMPLIMENTS

Another difference which can lead to a battle between the sexes is in the area of giving compliments. There is a classic scene in the documentary film about Madonna, *In Bed with Madonna*, where Kevin Costner comes backstage to meet her after her performance. Anyone watching the film of Madonna performing on stage could not help feeling uplifted. She is open, sexually uninhibited and highly disciplined, and has a tremendously energetic style. The adjective to describe Madonna or one of her concerts is anything but 'Neat', as Kevin Costner comments in a rather monotonous, boring tone when he goes to greet her.

Madonna becomes so turned off and disgusted by his lack of expression – his lack of verbal passion – that when he leaves the room she sticks her finger down her throat as though she were gagging and says, 'Neat, what a jerk!' Had he said 'Incredible', 'Phenomenal', 'Fantastic' or 'Sensational', he would have been held in greater esteem not only by Madonna but by everyone else who watched the film. What she was responding to in his behaviour was, unfortunately, an all too 'male' communication problem – being mean with compliments.

Non-expression is a turn-off, as Sally discovered. Sally spent several hours getting ready for a special evening with her husband, Todd. She had her hair trimmed and styled. She was manicured, pedicured, massaged and given a facial. She spent ages picking the right outfit. Finally she decided on her indigo blue dress, which other people said made her look sensational.

When Todd finally arrived home from work she opened the door and smiled. But suddenly her bright smile turned into a tight frown when she heard Todd say in a monotonous, boring tone, 'You look nice.'

Sally replied, in a rather hostile tone, 'If you don't like the way I look, why don't I go upstairs and change?'

'Why?' said Todd, dumbfounded. 'I said you looked nice . . . what do you want me to do, turn cartwheels?'

No, Todd. Sally doesn't want you to turn cartwheels. All she wants you to do is tell her how phenomenal she looks. 'You look nice' is not enough. Men need to be more descriptive and use more intensifiers, like 'so', 'really' or 'very'. They should use more adjectives, and say something like, 'You look great!' or 'Darling, I really love the way you put yourself together tonight. You look so sexy in that gorgeous blue dress – it really brings out the colour of your eyes. You look so gorgeous – and that dress really shows off your sexy body!' Had Todd said any of these things he would certainly not have been met with a frown and a cold reaction. Most likely he would have had a hug and a kiss, and the evening would have got off to a much better start.

Men must use adjectives and descriptions when talking to women, because this is how women have been conditioned. Men must take the time to observe, and then express what they observe. It is unacceptable for a man to withhold compliments from a woman. Instead, he needs to express himself freely and clearly, without feeling embarrassed or uncomfortable not only about giving compliments but about receiving them as well.

Men need to forget about their uncomfortable feelings and realize that women deeply appreciate being complimented. A man needs to look closely at what he sees. He needs to look at the colour, the style and the texture of what the woman is wearing. He needs to hear the sounds and tones of the woman's voice. He needs to feel the texture of her hair and skin. He needs to smell her perfume. In short, he needs to express what all of his senses are experiencing if he wants to communicate to the fullest extent with a woman.

I shared this information with one of my clients, who immediately started to apply these techniques to his wife. He noticed an enormous change in how she responded to him. In fact, he told me that she had become a lot more affectionate whenever he expressed himself in the way I taught him.

When a couple compliment one another, it is very important to be honest and sincere in complimenting the person in areas in which they are deserving. Otherwise your partner will detect your phoneyness and feel even worse than if you had said nothing. Both men and women need to compliment their partners often – even to notice the slightest accomplishment or improvement with a verbal pat on the back. This makes your partner feel as if you are more attentive and more appreciative of him or her.

IS THAT AN ORDER?

Another way in which men and women fail to communicate with one another is in the way they make requests. Many of us have experienced a version of the following scenario.

Dan and Mary both work hard and are usually exhausted when they come home. After a tense day at the office, Dan plopped down on the sofa, turned on the television and then yelled to Mary, who was in the kitchen, 'Get me a beer!'

Mary shouted back from the kitchen in a hostile tone, 'Get it yourself! Who do you think I am, your maid?'

Her retort completely stunned Dan, who had never expected such a hostile response. He replied, 'What's the matter with you? Do you have PMT or something? All I asked was for a lousy can of beer. Is that too much to ask for?'

'First of all, I don't have PMT. And secondly, no, it is not too much to ask for,' said Mary in a sharp tone. 'I don't appreciate your *ordering* me around.'

Had Dan said, 'Mary, could you possibly get me a beer, please?' or 'Darling, since you're in the kitchen could you get me a beer? I'd really appreciate it.' Then he would not only be drinking his can of beer but he might even find himself eating a sandwich that Mary might have prepared for him. But his commanding made Mary feel like pouring the beer on his head and shoving the sandwich down his throat. Men have no idea how barking out a command or a request hurts a woman's feelings.

If they are to bridge the communication gap, men must realize that there is no need to bark out commands. If you want to maintain any kind of committed relationship with a woman you need to incorporate into your conversation terms of endearment such as 'Darling', as well as those of politeness, such as saying, 'Would you mind?' or 'Please'. 'Please' is an essential word when communicating.

If you use more terms of endearment with women and also more emotional phrases such as 'I love the way . . .', 'I feel like . . .', 'It hurts me when . . .', 'I'm excited about . . .', 'I feel sad when . . .', or 'It makes me so happy when . . .', you will probably elicit a warm, attentive response from the woman you are with. In this way you will be speaking her language, which can help close that communication gap.

LETTING YOUR FEELINGS OUT

One of the major differences between men and women concerns how they let their emotions out. When men let off steam due to anger and frustration they tend to shout; women, on the other hand, often cry. There is nothing wrong with either of these two ways. If you have to express yourself, don't be afraid to do so.

Anna Maria, one of my clients, grew up in an Italian family where screaming and yelling was a way of life. So she thought nothing of letting someone 'have it' verbally in a loud, rich, fast-talking voice. She was very conscientious about paying her bills, and after getting the run-around for six months about an allegedly unpaid bill which had actually been paid, she went to the store in question to sort things out. After telling her story and being shuffled to three different people, she felt that she had had enough. So in a loud, booming voice she said, 'Look, I'm sick of you people! Get your acts together! I want to speak to the manager. I never want to do business here again, and I want to close my account.'

Even though her shouting stunned the entire room and embarrassed the employees, she did get results. The supervisor came in and apologetically handled her problem. So don't be afraid to let out your emotions and raise your voice when the situation warrants it.

MEN, DON'T BE AFRAID TO CRY

Crying is another SEX TALK DIFFERENCE that needs to be explored in terms of letting out emotions. There is no reason why a man who is feeling extremely frustrated or overwhelmed can't let off steam through tears, just as a woman can release her frustrations through shouting. But men do not open up as much as women – they tend to hold more of their feelings inside. This is no secret. Studies show that men disclose less personal information about themselves than women, especially when they are hurt, angry or emotionally overwhelmed.

Trevor, a thirty-two-year-old client of mine who is a salesman, told me of the following incident. His girlfriend gave him a birthday present – an appointment with a psychic. Although he was quite sceptical and thought the idea ridiculous, he quickly changed his attitude when the psychic revealed more and more accurate personal information about him, telling him things that nobody would have known – not even his girlfriend. After relaying these experiences, Trevor said, 'You know, when I left the psychic I wanted to cry. But I didn't . . . I couldn't.'

When I asked him why not, he replied, 'Well, I had to go back to work, and I didn't want all the guys to see me with a red and puffy face and hear them say, "Hey, you've been *crying*?" and start joking around and poking fun at me.' How unfortunate it was for Trevor that he couldn't cry because of peer pressure. Unfortunately, he is not alone. There are many men who have been sensitized to peer pressure ever since they were children.

Another one of my clients, Brian, told me how as a boy he quickly learned never to cry. As a ten-year-old, he cried because some of the other boys were bullying a disabled boy with braces on his legs by pushing and shoving him. Brian tried to stop them but couldn't, and was so frustrated that he began to cry. For the rest of his schooldays he was labelled a crybaby and a sissy, which immediately put an end to his tears – at least in public. Fortunately for Brian, he has now grown up and has since been able to shed both tears of joy and tears of sadness.

An actor client of mine, who played the role of Billy Bigalow in the musical *Carousel*, told me how men consistently stifled their tears. In one scene in the play this actor has to die on stage. For what seemed to him like an eternity he had to lie on the floor without moving. With his eyes closed as he attempted to portray a dead person, his hearing became even more acute. In the audience he clearly heard sniffling, noses being blown and tears, which he assumed were coming from the women. He also heard a lot of low-pitched throaty 'uhm-mmm' sounds from the men in the audience, who were making these noises in order to stifle their emotions and hold back their tears.

The myth that little boys shouldn't cry and that men have to be strong is just that – a myth. Men *need* to cry when they feel frustrated or emotional in order to let off steam. When tears are released, chemicals are released which help reduce stress. Crying not only allows you to release tension but also lets you express all those pent-up emotions you feel in your daily personal life. As human beings we all need to feel our emotions, and we should not be afraid to let out our tears when we feel them. This human vulnerability of letting out true emotions makes a person very appealing to the opposite sex, which further helps to bridge that gap.

OPENING UP, CONFRONTING AND SELF-DISCLOSURE

Another difference between the ways in which men and women communicate is in how they open up and express things about themselves. In her book *Woman and Love, A Cultural Revolution in Progress* Shere Hite found that, in nearly 71 per cent of long-term marriages, women gave up communicating with their husbands and no longer tried to encourage them to talk. Her finding is quite distressing.

In *Why Can't Men Open Up?* Steven Naifeh and Gregory Smith came up with a term called 'manspeak', which they called 'part English, part code and part sign language'. They say that in 'manspeak' there is no little or no emotion, no excitement nor intensity, with a monotone of simple 'yups' and 'nopes' which makes the man appear more closed and uncommunicative.

Naifeh and Smith explain how frustrated women become when they try to communicate with an uncommunicative man. Often, women simply give up. All too often men don't respond because they really don't know how to have a conversation with a woman.

Jean spent the day with her travel agent, looking at brochures of various places that she thought she and her husband, Harold, might go to for their holiday. That evening she was very excited and proceeded to tell Harold about the exciting place she had discovered.

Jean Darling, I'm so excited – I've found a wonderful place for our holiday. It's right up in the mountains and the travel agent's offering a really good package.

Harold *(in a monotonous voice)* That's nice.

Because of Harold's lack of enthusiasm, Jean felt distanced. She felt that
  (a) he didn't like the place she had found,
  (b) he didn't want to go on holiday with her,
  (c) he was not interested in her,
  (d) he was cross with her, or
  (e) all of these.
The result was that Jean's feelings were hurt. Harold, on the other hand, thought it was great that she had done all the work on finding a holiday spot for them, and he really appreciated it. But while Jean was speaking to him his brows were knitted and his lips were tight because he had been thinking about a lawyer's letter he had received that day. His wife, however, interpreted Harold's facial expressions as negativity and anger. This is a clear example of how 'manspeak' – not opening up and saying what's on one's mind – can create miscommunication and potential

alienation. Had the following conversation taken place, no hard feelings would have had a chance to come up.

Jean   Darling, I'm so excited. I've found a wonderful place for our holiday. It's right up in the mountains and the travel agent's offering a really good package.

Harold I'm really pleased about that, Jean love. But can we discuss it later rather than just now, because I'm so preoccupied with this letter I got from my lawyer today that I'm feeling a bit anxious.

Now Jean has some idea about why Harold has a stern look on his face. She knows it has nothing to do with her. By opening up to Jean, Harold lets her into his feelings. This is the best way for couples to avoid potential misunderstandings. Unfortunately, all too often men have been conditioned not to express or confront their feelings; therefore, it is often difficult to change without some help and encouragement.

In a survey I conducted of a hundred males and a hundred females between the ages of eighteen and seventy-four, I found that men are not as apt to confront problems in their relationships or in their personal lives as readily as woman are. I asked the question, 'If you had a problem in your relationship, would you be the first to bring attention to it?' Close to 80 per cent of the men answered no, while 90 per cent of the woman said yes.

This also applies to confronting health issues as Dr Maxine Ostrum of Beverly Hills points out: 'A man will oftentimes wait until the last minute to come in with a serious medical problem, while a woman will come in to get help a lot sooner.' Men have a tendency to feel that, if they ignore the problem, it will go away. In the case of actor Michael Landon, this proved fatal. Michael found out much too late that he had liver and pancreatic cancer and died at the relatively young age of fifty-four. Had he confronted his health problem earlier, he might possibly have been alive to talk about it today.

Besides not confronting health issues, men do not bring up problem issues as often as women will – their attitude is that the problem will simply disappear if they ignore it. But by ignoring issues, men allow their personal problems to fester like cancer until they are beyond repair. It is essential for men to learn to confront and handle problems immediately in order to help close the communication gap between the sexes.

WAYS TO ENCOURAGE OPENING UP

Encourage openness by asking your partner how he feels about things. Then be attentive to what he has to say. Don't belittle feelings or discount them by saying such things as 'There's nothing to be afraid of' or 'Don't be ridiculous.' Opening up is not something that happens overnight. Men will usually have a difficult time expressing emotion because of their years of conditioning not to do so.

Also, you need to ask direct questions which are openended – for example, 'What was the greatest time you ever had when you were growing up?', 'What were your friends like when you were at school?', 'What was the funniest thing you ever did when you were a child?', or 'What kind of a teenager were you?' In this way you can encourage the flow of conversation.

Try these techniques for nine months to a year. If after this time you are continually frustrated with your partner's lack of openness, and you still want to continue the relationship, I suggest you both see a professional counsellor to help you learn how to communicate better with one another. You may have communication blocks with a more deep-rooted base, not necessarily related to the simple fact that men do not open up as much as women do.

One other point needs to be remembered. When getting a partner to open up and share secrets, it is important always to respect the confidences that are shared with you.

SUBJECTS OF INTEREST

Another way for women to get a man to open up is to bring up subjects that might interest him, such as sports, business or news events. Do this even if these topics are not particularly interesting to you.

If the man still continues to give one-word responses, such as 'Yup' or 'Nope', maintain direct eye contact and confront him about whether something is wrong. For example, ask him if he's angry with you or with someone else. If the answer is 'No', be direct and tell him that you find it very hurtful and disrespectful to have a conversation with someone who is not responsive. By expressing yourself and being direct, you can often ward off hard feelings and avoid any miscommunication.

FREE-FLOW CONVERSATION

When you begin to open up and get closer to another person, the real you eventually comes out. No matter how mundane or stupid a thought is, if you want to say it go ahead and do so. Almost everything you say is a reflection of what you're thinking about and who you are at that particular moment. If you don't censor yourself, you can create intimacy and trust. You also will get to know your partner even better.

For example, Renée and Mark were driving in the country when a flock of birds flew over them. The following conversation ensued:

Renée Sometimes I wish I was a bird.
Mark That's stupid – why would anyone want to be a bird?
Renée I don't think it's stupid.
Mark Actually, I'd like to be able to fly. I'd like to feel free and have total freedom. That *would* be nice!
Renée Can you imagine not having any responsibilities, not having to worry about the kids, your job, the bills, house payments and me? If you were a bird, you wouldn't have to worry about any of these things.
Mark Yes, but on the other hand, life wouldn't be as exciting without you.

As you can see, by bringing up a free-flowing uncensored thought Renée was able to encourage conversation with Mark, who was eventually able to disclose how he really felt.

DON'T ACCUSE, NAG OR BLAME

There will always be things that bother one of the parties in a relationship. If this occurs, be direct and open without destroying the other person's self-esteem.

Even if you are annoyed and frustrated about what your partner has done, it is essential that you don't berate him or her or fight like siblings. Although women tend to be more accusatory than men, men are more direct in their accusations ('You didn't call') whereas women are indirect

('Why didn't you call?'). Whether your accusation is direct or indirect, accusing and blaming are no way to encourage a harmonious relationship. First of all, no matter whether you are a man or a woman you need to be upfront and open without accusing the other person or using sharp, whining tones. Instead of saying, 'Why do you never take *me* anywhere – you're always out with your friends', you need to attribute your feelings to yourself and use 'I' instead of 'You'. A more profitable choice, which could result in a more positive reaction from your partner, would be, 'I feel so sad that we never go out any more' or 'I'd like to spend more time with you.' In essence, you need to describe how the person's actions are affecting you instead of attacking or putting him or her on the defensive.

ASKING FOR HELP

Comedienne Elaine Boosler has a great joke about men when it comes to their asking for help. She says, 'My ancestors wandered lost in the wilderness for forty years. The reason why is because, even in biblical times, men wouldn't stop to ask for directions.'

Ms Boosler's joke is all too true. Men are notorious for not asking for help, especially when they need directions. They'd much rather travel miles and miles trying to figure it out on their own than admit they are lost. This is one of the biggest complaints women make against men, as Deborah Tannen points out in *You Just Don't Understand*.

Perhaps childhood conditioning has something to do with this tendency. Little boys are taught to be independent and not to act like sissies or babies by constantly requesting help. But even though this appears to be a 'manly' thing to do, in reality it is not. If a man needs help or assistance, he needs to ask for it.

If women understand that this merely is one of the 'sex differences' in communication, they can help their man to realize it is OK to ask for help. Instead of arguing, you can say, 'I know you'd like to work this out on your own, and you probably have a good sense of direction, but I'd prefer it if we could stop and ask someone the way.' By saying this you are allowing the man to save face, as you are now talking in his language. In essence, you are allowing him to help you by honouring your feelings of discomfort about the matter.

IT'S NOT FUNNY –
STOP JOKING AROUND

Men and women definitely find different things funny, which can affect the way they communicate. One of the biggest complaints women have is that they don't like men's jokes; and all too often, men accuse women of having no sense of humour. One reason why women don't think male-oriented jokes are funny is because to a large extent male jokes are sexist. A recent study of male humour counted a ratio of twenty jokes about women to every one about men.

Male humour seems to involve more practical joking, such as nailing people's shoes to the floor, making apple pie beds or making fun of a person – how they look, how they act – or about members of their family. Furthermore, men will often joke about a woman's anatomy, which most women don't find particularly funny. Perhaps little boys are more conditioned to play practical jokes and tease one another, as this is learned at school with their peers. A popular boy is one who can take a joke – that is, who can tolerate the teasing and not be upset by it.

Raul was born in El Salvador and moved to Los Angeles with his parents when he was eight. He was born with a hare lip, which left an unsightly scar running from his upper lip up to his nose. When he first arrived at school his teacher noticed that none of the children were friendly to him. During break one day, a group of boys decided to tease Raul unmercifully. This went on for a week, until one day the teacher observed an older boy taunting Raul about his scar. He said to Raul, 'Hey, ugly, what happened to that lip of yours?' Another boy immediately chimed in, 'Yeah, what's that gross thing?' Raul looked up directly at the boys, smiled and said, 'Oh, that! I cut myself shaving this morning!' The older boys started to laugh along with Raul, and after that incident he was never teased again. In fact, Raul became the most popular child at the school. Perhaps his humour was what the other boys found so appealing.

It is a lot different with girls. When girls are teased, they tend to take it a lot more personally. They will often cry and tell their teacher. If they are constantly teased, they may regress and become painfully shy. In essence, little boys learn to develop a tougher skin than little girls.

Girls are also conditioned not to laugh at crude jokes which are not 'ladylike'. In fact, what is considered 'ladylike' is passed down from one generation to the next. At one time even laughing out loud was considered 'un-ladylike' behaviour.

Women do not like to hear jokes negating their sex, such as those about women drivers, mothers-in-law or dumb blondes. In a 1989 poll of three thousand American women over half found these types of jokes annoying. Put another way, slightly less than half stated they were not at all bothered by this type of humour. This may indicate that some women have developed a thicker skin and are immune to this kind of offensiveness. Or perhaps women are somewhat chauvinistic themselves and have accepted these sexual stereotype jokes.

When a woman tries to imitate raunchy 'male' humour she is not as well accepted and is often booed, hissed or silenced off the stage, as was the case of a comedienne I heard performing not long ago. Similarly, if a man makes the mistake and shares raunchy humour with a woman, he will usually not get a positive reaction. Often, the woman will think less of the man.

Men seem to be more sarcastic than women and to tease more because they seem to be more uncomfortable about opening up. By making kidding remarks or teasing they don't have to confront an issue in an open and direct manner, as the story of Stephen and Rita illustrates.

The couple were having a pleasant dinner at a restaurant when Rita ordered an extra side dish of pasta. Stephen commented, in a sarcastic tone and with a smile on his face, 'Sure, go ahead! While you're at it why don't you order another main course? Besides, you wanted some new clothes, and you might get them. It doesn't matter if they're a bigger size, does it?' Rita suddenly withdrew and felt embarrassed. Instead of laughing at the situation, she retreated and became sullen. However, Stephen thought he had been very clever and chuckled at his wit.

What he had really meant to say was that he cared about Rita, and didn't want her to feel guilty about gaining weight after she had worked so hard on her figure. Had he said, 'Darling, go ahead and eat whatever you want. But remember, this morning you were talking about how tight your clothes are getting. I only want to help,' then Stephen would not have created any hard feelings.

Men need to understand that teasing and sarcasm don't go down that well with women. On the other hand, if a man does slip, and he does use sarcasm or tease, women need to realize that it is a male SEX TALK DIFFERENCE. They should either go with the flow or let him know that they don't find what he says particularly funny and that his joke is not one that they can appreciate. If we *understand* that men and women have a completely different outlook on humour, we can avoid conflict between the sexes.

By educating your partner to appreciate that critical remarks can be hurtful, you will further enhance your communication. In so doing you can maintain more positive feelings towards one another, which can further help to close the communication gap.

CAN BETTER COMMUNICATION REDUCE DATE RAPE?

A lot has been written about the unfortunate subject of date rape. The statistics are astounding, and the problem is so serious that it recently merited a cover story in *Time* magazine. Records show that most college students who are raped knew the man who did it. And according to Mary Beth Rodin of the Santa Monica Rape Treatment Center, one out of every six female college students has been raped.

I would not wish to belittle the issue and its severity. But perhaps establishing better communication with the opposite sex might help combat the problem of date rape.

Little has changed over the past thirty years in terms of cultural norms as they apply to a first date. Studies in the non-verbal communication in traditional sex roles, done a few years ago by Suzanna Rose of the University of Missouri at St Louis and Irene Hanson Frieze of the University of Pittsburgh, found that most 'dating etiquette' is specific to one sex or the other, especially in the area of dominance and submission. Men are expected to initiate, plan and pay for the date; they are also the sexual aggressors. Women, on the other hand, are supposed to assume a subordinate role by being alluring, making conversation and 'limiting the sexual activity'.

Their findings suggest that 'male dominance' and control of dating persists during the first date. They also found that women were seen more as sexual objects and emotional facilitators, while men were regarded as planners, economic providers and sexual initiators. There would seem to be 'scripts' that these young women adhere to in regard to their dating roles. Perhaps there is a quality of acquiescence in women that is responsible for allowing many of these date rapes to occur.

Certainly this does not apply to all cases. But perhaps if young women were taught to be less tentative, less polite, more assertive and to the point, as indicated by the SEX TALK DIFFERENCES, as well as to be more direct in setting limits and less flirtatious, then perhaps date rape might be reduced to a great extent.

Mary Yarber, a high school counsellor and author of a recent article in the *Los Angeles Times* entitled 'First Year Students are at Greater Risk in On-Campus Rape', seems to support Rose and Frieze's conclusions. She states, 'If young women learn to communicate better, they can often help to reduce the chances of being sexually attacked.'

I agree wholeheartedly with her suggestion that young women need to learn to be more assertive in a clear, direct, unhesitating tone, as they have the right to say 'No' and the right to have their wishes respected. Even so, as Ms Yarber points out, it is difficult for women because so many of them have been taught to be passive and to defer to men, as verified by Rose and Frieze's study.

Several studies on victims of crime show that those who walk like a victim, with their heads down, a slow gait and poor posture, are more likely to be assaulted than those who project a more confident presence with head erect, good posture and a brisk stride. The same holds true for the tone of one's voice. How she says things, along with what she says, can often decide whether or not a woman is raped or whether she lives or dies. Women need to sound stronger by learning to resonate their tones; this is done by drawing out their vowels and using their abdominal muscles to project tones so they come over in a strong and assertive manner.

VOCAL SELF-DEFENCE

If a young woman does not want to have sex with a young man, it is important that she uses a strong, deep voice, appropriate body language, and a definite vocal tone to reflect that she is serious. As indicated in the SEX TALK DIFFERENCES, too many women come across as weak and tentative. Instead, in such a situation women need to maintain direct eye contact. They should take a breath in and then say in a loud, clear voice, without giggling and without tentative upward inflection, 'No, I am not interested in having sex with you. So please leave me alone.' This vocal defence technique can be invaluable in deterring potential date rapes.

HOW MEN CAN IMPROVE THEIR RELATIONSHIPS WITH WOMEN

Here is a recap of pointers, based on the 105 SEX TALK DIFFERENCES, to enable men to communicate better with women.

1 Have a more attentive body language when you are sitting down. Don't sit in a reclining position, which will make you look uninterested.

2   Hold your head straight up and don't tilt it to the side. When you do that, it makes you appear judgemental and defensive.

3   When you gesture while talking to a woman, try to make your gestures closer to your body. This will make you appear more intimate and sensitive.

4   Be more conscious of how much room and space you take up while sitting or standing, so you don't appear rude and intrusive to a woman. Sit closer to her (but not too close).

5   When you are talking to a woman on a personal level, don't fidget and rock back and forth. Not only is this distracting, but it gives her the impression that you are not interested in what she is saying. It will also convey the message that you are in a hurry and want to leave.

6   Look directly at a woman as you talk. That does not mean you should stare – just keep looking in her direction. Look at her entire face for a few seconds, then her eyes, nose, mouth, chin and finally her whole face again.

7   Smile more. If you're interested in someone, let them know.

8   When you talk to a woman, open your jaw when you speak. If you clench your jaw, you will appear uptight and uncommunicative. Also your tones will be more muffled, which can be very annoying.

9   Try to put enthusiasm into your voice when you greet and converse with a woman. A monotonous voice is not appealing.

10 In conversation, respond to topics which a woman brings up. Don't try to change the subject and don't interrupt. When you do this, it makes her feel as though you don't think what she has to say is important, and that you have little respect for her.

11 When listening to a woman, give her more immediate feedback when she's talking. Interject 'uhmmmms' and nod more. Doing this will make you appear more attentive and more interested in what she has to say.

12 When responding to a question a woman has asked you, don't give minimal responses like 'Yep', 'Nope' or 'Maybe'. Give a complete answer and then explain in greater detail why you said what you did.

13 In your descriptions, use more adjectives and intensifiers such as 'so', 'really', 'incredibly', 'vastly' and so forth. This will make you sound more interesting and interested. Paying attention in this way helps you appear more aware, observant, sensitive and perceptive.

14 When trying to stimulate conversation, ask the woman questions rather than going off on a monologue or a lecture. Let her talk and voice her opinions, too. Ask her about her 'feelings' on topics in order to keep up the momentum of the conversation. Doing so will make you appear more sensitive and more attentive.

15 Don't ever use command terms to a woman. Never say, 'Get me this or that.' If you are personally involved with a woman, be sure to couch your commands with terms of endearment such as 'darling', and phrase your words with politeness. 'Please' uttered in a pleasing, warm tone, is the key word if you don't want a woman to resent doing things for you.

16   On a similar note, never make a direct accusation to a woman if you want her to listen to what you are saying and if you don't want to 'turn her off'. Instead of saying, 'You haven't picked up the dog from the vet yet!' in an accusatory tone, you may want to couch your displeasure in the form of a question, using a more gentle tone with upward inflection, coupled with terms of endearment (for instance, 'Darling, was there some reason why you didn't pick up the dog from the vet?'). By doing this the woman is more apt to respond in a kind, positive manner and not defensively with a counter-attack.

17   Don't be stingy about giving a woman compliments. Be sincere, and use words that portray true excitement.

18   When you are frustrated, at your wits' end or emotionally moved, don't be afraid to let off steam not only through yelling and shouting but also through tears. It makes you appear more human and sensitive.

19   Save your dirty and practical jokes for your male friends. Women really don't appreciate this type of humour.

20   Don't use swear words. They usually offend women.

21   Learn to talk about personal issues. Don't be afraid to express yourself openly and honestly. Talk about subjects that women find more interesting such as self-improvement, clothes, other people and relationships.

22   Don't be afraid to ask for help when you need it.

HOW WOMEN CAN IMPROVE THEIR RELATIONSHIPS WITH MEN

From girlhood to adulthood, women tend to develop more socializing and more communicating behaviour patterns than men do. Therefore there are not as many things they need to do in order to improve their communication skills in their personal and social lives. However, here are a few pointers that women may find useful.

1   If you find a man being rude, sarcastic or insulting don't keep your feelings inside where they will fester. Express yourself openly and directly.

2   Don't let a man interrupt you. If he does, interject and say, 'Excuse me, I've not finished saying what I have to say.' If he persists and continues to interrupt, or if he changes the subject, say in a loud, firm voice, 'Excuse me, I was talking about such and such. Let's continue with the subject we were just talking about.'

3   Learn to feel more at ease talking about yourself and your accomplishments when you are asked about them. This will enable the man with whom you are talking to acquire a more realistic and true sense of who you are and what you're all about.

4   Watch your use of swear words, since this can put men off.

5   Don't be afraid to let a man know that you are angry.

6 Try to talk about more things that men enjoy discussing, such as sport, news events and cars.

7 Don't be afraid to approach a man and ask him out, especially if you are interested in him. Often it's appreciated. If he happens to reject you, don't personalize it and let it affect your self-esteem.

8 During arguments, don't bring up past problems. Stick to the particular issues at hand and try to resolve them.

9 If a man has problems opening up, don't push him to talk. Otherwise it sounds as if you're nagging, which most men hate. Let him know that, whenever he feels ready to talk, you will be ready to listen. Try to help him by asking more open-ended questions, encouraging more free-flowing conversation and talking about things he is interested in.

10 Don't drop your head down and look up when you talk. It makes you look subservient and victim-like. Instead, hold the crown of your head up as though there is an imaginary rope pulling it higher.

11 Try to bear down on your abdominal muscles when you talk, which helps to keep your voice pitch under control and a little lower. Besides making you sound more sensuous, it assists you in gaining more control over your voice if you are feeling anxious and nervous, particularly in social situations.

5

Closing the Communication Gap in Your Intimate Relationships

Of the 105 SEX TALK DIFFERENCES listed in Chapter 2 there appear to be thirty which apply to your love life. If not understood, they can have a damaging effect on this very personal area of man–woman relationships. Many of these differences are the same as those given in Chapter 4. However, in this context the application is different.

1 Men are not as sensitive to non-verbal communication cues as women are, which makes women appear more sensitive and intuitive.

2 Men initiate more touching than women do. As a result men are touched less often by women.

3 Men tend to be less gentle in touching others than women are.

4 Men approach women more closely in terms of invading their personal space.

5   Women make more direct eye contact and look at men directly, facing them, whereas men tend not to make as much direct eye contact and tend to look at the person from an angle. This is especially evident even during positive interactions with the opposite sex.

6   When providing intimate feedback and interactions, men exhibit less facial expression than women do.

7   Men exhibit less emotional warmth through facial animation than women do.

8   Men interrupt more, and allow fewer interruptions than women.

9   Men mumble more and have sloppier pronunciation than women, which could be a turn-off in the bedroom.

10   Women use more tones when they talk, making them sound more emotional, whereas men use fewer tones which makes them sound less emotional, less approachable and more abrupt.

11   Men disclose less personal information about themselves than women do.

12   Men and women make requests differently. Men make more direct commands, while women are less direct and use more terms of endearment.

13   Men are more silent during conversational lulls, whereas women will interject some word such as 'uhm-mmm' to keep the conversation connected and going. Men also provide less feedback during conversation.

14 Men use fewer psychological and emotional state verbs than women do.

15 Men answer questions by offering minimal responses: 'Yep', 'OK', 'No', 'Fine', and use fewer adjectives and descriptive statements than women do.

16 Men use fewer adjectives of adoration (such as 'adorable', 'charming', 'precious' and 'sweet') than women do. Men also use fewer terms of endearment.

17 Women are less blunt and more diplomatic than men.

18 Men ask fewer questions than women to stimulate conversation.

19 Men use stronger expletives and more slang words than women.

20 Men tend to lecture more and conduct a monologue rather than a dialogue than women.

21 Men give fewer compliments than women.

22 Men use more teasing and sarcasm to show affection, whereas women are more openly direct in this context. Men also tell cruder and more sexually oriented jokes.

23 Women appear to be more intuitive as they pay more attention to details, whereas men tend to be less aware of details and so appear to be less intuitive.

24 Men have more difficulty in expressing intimate feelings and emotions than women.

25 Women tend to censor their thoughts less than men and to communicate more through a stream of consciousness.

26 Women differ from men in the way they argue. Women hold more grudges and bring up things from the past, while men hold fewer grudges and mostly stick to the problem in hand.

27 Men are more task-oriented and discuss what they physically did and what they are going to do. On the other hand women tend to talk more about how they feel about what they did and what they are about to do.

28 Men and women apologize differently. Men find more difficulty in apologizing than women, and when men apologize they use less emotion.

29 Women talk more about relationships than men do.

30 Men feel less comfortable than women when they hear accolades and praise about themselves.

After reading these SEX TALK DIFFERENCES, it is not surprising that men and women have difficulty communicating with one another in the bedroom.

When making love:

1 Do you always tell your partner what you want him or her to do?

2 Do you enjoy having your partner talk dirty to you?

3 Before lovemaking, are you open to discussing sexually transmitted diseases, AIDS and safe sex?

4   Are you uninhibited about trying new sexual experiences?

5   Do you give your partner any feedback as to whether or not you are enjoying what you are doing?

If you answered 'No' to any of these questions, you are not alone. I have surveyed hundreds of people who have given the same response.

Most couples are inhibited about communicating with one another while making love. It is such a paradox that two people can be physically close yet cannot bring themselves to talk about their physical closeness. Despite the sexual revolution of the sixties and seventies we are still 'communicatively frigid' and 'verbally impotent'. Reading this chapter will help you establish a new sexual intimacy through communication.

MAKING LOVE THROUGH YOUR FACE AND BODY LANGUAGE

Do you remember the first James Bond movies, starring Sean Connery? He would passionately grab his love interest, hold her close to his hairy chest, look deeply into her eyes, pout his sensuous lips and then give her the most breathtaking kiss of her life. What was it that got our blood pumping and our hearts beating so rapidly as we watched Mr Bond in action?

It was his charisma and confidence. Sean Connery's body language and facial expression told us that he was sexy. In fact, it is no accident that a few years ago *People* magazine voted him the Sexiest Man Alive – even though he was sixty at the time!

What makes Sean Connery and a whole host of others – Gérard Depardieu, Mickey Rourke, Mel Gibson, Kathleen Turner, Andie McDowell and Kim Basinger – have sex appeal? It's not just the way they look; it's how they look at their on-screen lovers when they are making love to them.

You too can have the same attributes by learning how to incorporate the SEX TALK DIFFERENCES during love-making, such as looking directly into your lover's eyes when you talk to them and when you are intimate with them. You need to express your affection openly not just in a physical way but verbally too. You must be sensitive not only to your lover's needs but also to his or her emotional concerns.

INTIMACY THROUGH TOUCH

Physical affection is essential if you are to have a fulfilling, intimate relationship. Couples need to feel comfortable holding hands, touching one another and putting their arms around each other. Touching is an essential part of intimacy. It's also another way in which men and women communicate with each other.

Men touch women more often than vice versa. It is usually the man who first puts his arms around a woman or who first reaches out to touch her hand. When they are only casually acquainted, women tend to be annoyed by men who touch them freely. This may be because women don't feel the man's touch is very sincere. So whenever a man touches a woman he needs to be honest about his intentions – does he really like her, or is he merely being flirtatious? In the latter case, men should keep their hands to themselves.

Too many women have been turned off by men who have 'fishlike handshakes' or 'fishlike touches', as they describe them. These women make comments like 'They give me the creeps', 'They feel disgusting' or 'They're wimps.' If a man is going to touch a woman, that touch has to be firm and welcomed. If a woman recoils you can rest assured that she doesn't want your hands near her. Men need to be sensitive about these non-verbal signals, especially when trying to establish an intimate relationship.

Daniella finally went out with a man whom several people had wanted her to meet. They had a very nice first date and all went well until he walked her to her door. She was completely turned off when he touched her and tried to kiss her goodnight. She commented, 'He gave me the creeps. I hated the way he touched me and even more so the way he kissed – so I decided to forget him.'

On the other hand, if a woman is interested in a man she needs to let him know it, and not be afraid to reach out and touch him. I recently invited two friends to my house for dinner because I wanted them to meet one another. It was apparent within the first five minutes that the woman, Cynthia, was very attracted to the man, Gary. She let him know this by freely touching his forearm as she told him a funny story. Throughout dinner, she maintained her tactile communication with him. It was fortunate that Gary felt the same way as he reciprocated her touches. The dinner was definitely a success, as the two of them subsequently began dating.

Dr David Givens, an anthropologist at the University of Washington, has conducted studies on non-verbal body language during courtship. He found that, when a woman is interested in a man, she will usually respond to a man's touch by grabbing his forearm when telling a story in order to express her interest in him. Dr Givens states that in social situations, if partners are compatible, they will mutually exchange a series of affectionate gestures by way of 'accidentally touching one another'. He observes that a man will often pick a hair off a woman's blouse or admire her watch as he takes hold of her wrist to comment about it. In turn Dr Givens states, the woman will touch the man's arm to let him know that she likes him back. So if a woman touches a man after he touches her, she is probably attracted to him.

When relationships go beyond their early stages and an intimate bond is formed, most women crave physical closeness. Perhaps, as babies and little girls, they are touched more often than little boys. Men need to be aware of this, and to touch and cuddle often. In fact, studies have shown that women enjoy cuddling and snuggling with men as much as they enjoy having sexual intercourse.

If a man is not as touch-oriented as a woman would like him to be, she needs to educate him in a loving manner by saying something like, 'It makes me feel so good when you hold and touch me.' It is also extremely important to let your partner know how and where you like to be touched, not just during sex but even when you are holding hands or when your partner has his or her arms around you. People's preferences vary: some like a hard touch, while others like a soft, more feathery one. The key is to communicate what you like and to feel free to say what is on your mind.

Couples who have been together for a long time and have a solid relationship have learned exactly how to touch their partner. Often their body movements have become so much in tune that each partner knows what the other is feeling and thinking just by the special language of their touch. Couples who touch one another often have greater physical intimacy in their marriage than those who don't touch as much. Couples who touch more are also perceived as being a lot closer emotionally and more attentive to one another. Research has also indicated that married couples who sit closer to one another and touch one another tend to report happier marriages than those couples who don't do these things. So if you want to have a closer, more intimate relationship with your partner you need to reach out and touch them, and make sure your

93

touch reflects how you really feel. Having a firm, solid grip (though not too hard) will help let the other person know you are interested in and connected with them.

A BODY POSTURE THAT TURNS YOUR PARTNER ON

Aside from a person's touch, their body posture and movement are critical in enhancing intimate communication between couples. One real turn-off is a person who has a stiff and uptight posture. On the other hand, a person with a loose, comfortable body posture is perceived as being more secure, open and warm, which usually translates as such in the bedroom.

If you want to communicate more sensuously with the opposite sex, you must first lighten up and loosen any rigid body movement. Consciously relaxing will help you eliminate any fears you may have about touching another person and being touched by the other person.

INTIMATE EYES AND EARS

A great lover is someone who pays such close attention to their partner's needs that he or she can tell how tense or upset their partner is just by observing their facial expressions or even the tension in their neck. Because they are so perceptive and so ready to please their partner, they may think nothing of giving him or her a spontaneous neck massage even when it isn't asked for. Women tend to be naturally more receptive and sensitive to their partners' facial expressions; by being aware of this SEX TALK

DIFFERENCE men too can make a conscious effort to become more aware of women's non-verbal and body language cues.

Debra, one of my clients, told me that one of the things she loved most about her husband was that he could understand her needs by reading her facial expressions and body cues. While she was making dinner after a horrible, tense day, her husband placed his hands on the back of her neck and proceeded to rub out the knot he felt. She was so appreciative that she responded to him sexually, and the two of them had the best lovemaking session she had ever experienced on the kitchen counter. Because of his unselfish giving, she was able to give back and express her gratitude through lovemaking.

Men who want to achieve greater intimacy with their partners should pay close attention and observe their reactions. They also need to remember the important things their partner tells them – such as the fact that she likes silver roses – and, in turn, surprise her with a bouquet of them. Or on her birthday they should invite her best friends over to a surprise party. Women tend to be better observers anyway; men who are looking for better communication should learn to pay greater attention to these details in order to enhance intimacy with their partner.

If, as some say, the eyes are the windows to the soul, then you need to look directly into your partner's eyes to establish intimacy through communication; men find more difficulty than women in doing this. You even need to look at your partner when she enters a room. I often hear women complain that their man doesn't even acknowledge them when they enter a room, and as a result they feel taken for granted.

Some men just call out, 'Hello, darling. I'm home,' as they drop their briefcase on the floor, then plop down in an armchair to read the newspapers. They don't think to search the house to find their wife, hold her close, look into her eyes and lovingly kiss her. These men are missing out on what intimate communication is all about. No matter how busy or overwhelmed you are, men in particular need to make it a priority to greet their partner each time they enter a room. You don't have to hug and kiss, but you do have to acknowledge your partner by your warm tone, warm smile, warm gaze and direct eye contact.

INTIMATE EYE CONTACT

Since men have more of a problem in this area, as indicated in the SEX TALK DIFFERENCES, they must work hard on maintaining eye contact, especially during lovemaking. Looking into one another's eyes also helps break down any defences between you, as it allows you to relate to your partner on a deeper and more passionate level.

In the movies, we have seen how our favourite screen lovers gaze deeply into one another's eyes, anxiously waiting to turn their romantic fantasies into sensual realities. Without realizing it, we may actually learn a lot from our on-screen heroes and heroines, who can teach us how to enjoy more intimacy in our communication with our real-life loves.

For a woman there is nothing more disconcerting than making love to a man who does not look directly at her or who gives her virtually no eye contact. This happened to a client of mine, Britt, who noticed that her fiancé was in the habit of not looking at her while they were making love. After experiencing hurt feelings for long enough she finally told him how awful and alienated she felt. She told him that it affected her ability to respond to him sexually, as she had difficulty in letting herself go. When he didn't look at her, she felt that all he really cared about was his own sexual satisfaction, and that he could not care less about her.

Her fiancé was shocked, as he had no idea how she felt. After taking heed and addressing Britt's need to be looked at while they made love, all her negative feelings disappeared. They subsequently found themselves experiencing an even deeper closeness.

YOUR VOICE AS A SEXUAL BAROMETER

We all have heard about love at first sight, but what about love at first sound? Studies show that the way a person sounds can be a sexual turn-on or turn-off during lovemaking.

Several years ago I conducted a survey for the Playboy Television Channel, in which I interviewed several men and women and asked them if they became sexually aroused by the tone of their partner's voice. Close to 95 per cent of the couples whom I interviewed told me they did. In a more recent survey I asked numerous men what type of voices they found sexy. It is no surprise that actress Kathleen Turner came out as number one. Most people agree, and many women have called my office asking me whether I could teach them how to sound like Kathleen Turner, Jane Fonda or Debra Winger. Most of the female callers realize that a low-pitched, elegant tone is sexy. Women in particular need to be conscious of their vocal tones, as a high-pitched, nasal tone can be a definite turn-off in the bedroom.

To acquire a low-pitched, sensuous voice, open up the back of your throat and your jaws and bear down with your stomach muscles. To have a sexy voice, keep the volume of your voice down when talking to your partner. To have a soft tone, take in a small sip of air through your lips; then feel the smooth air flowing out, passing from the back of your throat down into your abdominal area as you slowly exhale. Take your time drawing out your vowels to produce the soft, breathy words on a gentle airstream, especially when you are talking while making love.

Remember, too, that an expressive voice is also a sexy voice. This is especially important for men, who are often guilty of speaking in a flat monotone. You can say the most beautiful words imaginable to a woman, but if you're talking in a monotone there's a very good chance that these words won't be heard. In order to sound sexy and sincere, you need to put passion and emotion into your voice. Remember that the feelings in your heart often come out in your voice. If you stop putting a lid on your emotions when you speak, you will begin to say what you really feel; that will make you even more appealing to a woman.

Of all the vocal patterns, perhaps the biggest sexual turn-off is a monotonous, boring voice. Unfortunately, too many men are guilty of this: it makes them particularly unappealing to woman as it makes them sound so detached. How can a woman believe a monotonous, boring voice that flatly drones out, 'I love you' or 'You are the most beautiful woman I've ever known.' The first instinct is to think 'I don't believe it', as the voice doesn't reflect at all the emotion of what is being said. Therefore you need to put some life and expression into your voice, especially when you talk to your lover during lovemaking. Saying 'I love you' by drawing out the vowel sound in the word 'love' gives more meaning, as it enables you to show more passion.

Having a sexy-sounding voice is so powerful that someone listening to it can be turned on all the time, as my newly married client, Beverly, explained. She told me that she gets sexually excited whenever she hears her lover's deep, rich, sensuous, expressive voice or whenever she talks to him over the telephone. Since he travels a lot, his voice helps their love life while he is on the road.

Talking while making love can be a turn-on or a turn-off depending on what you say or don't say. Like good music, words and tones can arouse the emotions. In essence, creating a symphony of sexy tones can usually have an erotic effect upon your partner.

IT'S SEXY TO BE VULNERABLE – IT'S OK TO CRY

Men don't realize that they automatically become more appealing to women when they appear vulnerable and sensitive. Perhaps the clearest example of this can be seen in Sylvester Stallone's *Rocky I* character. Even though Rocky is a fighter, there is a sweet sensitivity about him. His vulnerability is reflected in the way he treats his girlfriend, Adrienne. This make Rocky seem even more lovable and endearing.

Despite this, many men are afraid to show their vulnerability through tears, as indicated in the list of SEX TALK DIFFERENCES. In a Harris Poll of a thousand men and women the following question was asked: 'When you really get angry or annoyed, how likely are you to cry?' According to the survey, only one hundred and eighty-three men answered affirmatively as compared to seven hundred and sixty-nine women. This difference clearly illustrates the disparity in the expression of emotion between men and women. Crying can be a great release of tension for both sexes. When couples shed tears with one another, all barriers are broken down and a stronger bond is formed.

One of my clients, Linda, told me that she felt much closer to her boyfriend after he had cried in her presence over a problem in their relationship. Larry was very jealous because Linda had had lunch with an old boyfriend.

Instead of being silent, he expressed the fact that he was afraid of losing her; then he broke down and cried. After doing so she saw him in a completely different light. She experienced a new dimension in their relationship which helped cement their love and subsequently led to their marriage.

ARGUMENTS DURING INTIMACY

I once watched a television programme in which a couple who had been married for over sixty years spoke about why they had such a successful marriage. Their secret was that they never went to bed angry: after an argument they made sure it was over by kissing and making up. This couple can teach us a lot. Intimate communication means not holding a grudge and not being afraid to disagree or argue. This information is especially important for women, since they have a greater tendency than men to hold on to a grudge and even to bring things up from the past.

According to studies, when men argue it is easier for them to get over it than it is for women. Men will often regard arguments as a contest that ends as soon as the arguing is over. After an argument, most men have little problem being affectionate and may even want to make love. As far as they are concerned the argument is over, and no hard feelings are left. Unfortunately, this is not so for most women. Women hold grudges longer because they frequently personalize arguments. Most women could not countenance making love to a man with whom they had just argued.

According to Dr H. G. Whittington of the University of Colorado in Denver, women do not see arguments as a contest with a beginning and an end. They consider issues that cause friction to be problems which flow continuously over time. As a result, most women believe there is nothing wrong with bringing up as ammunition something that may have happened a month or even ten years ago. Dredging up past problems can confuse and anger men: it is one of the major SEX TALK DIFFERENCES and can create a huge gap between men and women. Indeed, bringing up the past can often turn a minor argument into a full-scale battle.

When a man or woman starts an argument, he or she may be saying a lot more than the words spoken. It may be an attempt to communicate something much deeper than the immediate issue. For example, one of my clients, Cristy, told me how her husband was so tuned into her that he was able to see what was really bothering her.

She had been very angry with her husband for discouraging her from playing tennis because she was five months pregnant. Instead of telling him she was angry about this, she started an argument over his sloppiness and how he always left his clothes all over the bedroom. She began to berate him, got very upset and went through details of past experiences of tidying up after him. Finally her husband walked over to her, grabbed her by her shoulders, put his arms around her, held her close and said, 'Darling, I don't want to argue with you because I love you so much, and I don't want to win the argument. You're right – I *have* been messy. But I think something else is bothering you, so why don't we talk about it?'

She immediately broke down, started to cry, and admitted that she thought he was trying to control her like her father did. For years she had resented her father for always trying to interfere with her life. Then they discussed her husband's concern: there could be a problem if she was hit in the stomach by a tennis ball. Her husband told her he was merely expressing his love for both her and their unborn baby.

As you can see, even while arguing it's important to examine the true problem. Stop for a moment, then take a breath and really analyze what it is that you are arguing about. You may find it has nothing to do with the present issue but concerns something deeper.

No matter what, when you're angry about sexual issues argue fairly. Be sensitive and respect your partner's feelings. Never put your partner down by saying things like 'It's too weird' or 'That's such a stupid thing to do.' Your partner will feel extremely insecure and defensive. Here, too, stick to the immediate issue and don't bring up the past when criticizing your partner.

DOES YOUR PARTNER SAY WHAT YOU WANT TO HEAR IN BED?

In a Gallup Poll I commissioned for this book one thousand and eighteen men and women of eighteen years old and over, from across America, were asked their opinions of their partners' communication style during sex. The results showed that, overall, men and women felt the same: a similar (and shockingly low) proportion of both sexes are not satisfied with what they hear in bed. Only 34 per cent of the men like what they hear, while slightly fewer women, 28 per cent, are pleased with their bedroom conversation.

When asked if their partners did not say the things they wanted to hear, more women than men responded affirmatively: 116 out of 489 women answered 'Yes' to this question as compared to 81 out of the 497 men. In fact, more males agreed that they were indeed hearing what they wanted to hear from their partners; more than half of the men surveyed (264) responded that they were pleased with what they heard from women.

One out of every six adults feels that their partners talk too little during lovemaking. More men (18.8 per cent) than women (only 13.9 per cent) feel this way.

Out of all those surveyed, 14 per cent expressed the view that their partners did not display enough emotion. In this area racial differences are found. The lack of perceived 'emotionality' in their male partner was most significantly evident among non-caucasian women: 30 per cent of the non-caucasian women, as compared to 11 per cent of the caucasian women surveyed, responded that their partners were not very emotional when making love. Perhaps this relates to the SEX TALK DIFFERENCE which states that men are less emotional or use fewer psychological state verbs.

A small percentage of men and women felt that their partner wasn't serious enough in bed. In the survey, only 7 per cent of both men and women said that their partner talked too much during sex. This was found to be more prevalent among unmarried couples (10 per cent) than married (14 per cent). Even though SEX TALK DIF-FERENCES indicate that men talk more than women, it is interesting that younger men between the ages of eighteen and twenty-four are more likely to feel that their women partners talk too much (19 per cent). This is not, however, evident in younger women (7 per cent). Perhaps younger men don't yet realize that good communication is a pre-requisite to good lovemaking.

Here is a summary of the actual Gallup Poll results, where four hundred and ninety-seven men and four hundred and eighty-nine women were asked the following question.

Which of the following, if any, do you experience during sexual relations with your partner of the opposite sex? Based on those with a partner of the opposite sex, according to sex.

	MALE	FEMALE
Total number of men and women asked	497	489

Partner's behaviour

	MALE	FEMALE
Talks too much	69 8.9%	39 4.7%
Talks too little	145 18.8%	114 3.9%
Doesn't say the things you want to hear	81 10.4%	116 14.1%
Says the things you want to hear	264 34.1%	227 27.5%
Is not serious enough	65 8.4%	53 6.4%
Is not emotional enough	108 14.0%	111 13.5%
None of these	141 18.2%	137 16.6%
Don't know/refused	105 13.6%	159 19.3%
Not having/never had sexual relations	17 2.1%	40 4.9%

Which of the following, if any, do you experience during sexual relations with your partner of the opposite sex?

Based on those with a partner of the opposite sex, according to race.

	MALE		FEMALE	
	WHITE	NON-WHITE	WHITE	NON-WHITE
Total number of men and women asked	436	53	427	52
Partner's behaviour				
Talks too much	53 8.0%	13 14.0%	29 4.0%	10 9.8%
Talks too little	111 16.8%	29 30.7%	99 14.0%	14 13.9%
Doesn't say the things you want to hear	70 10.5%	11 11.5%	98 13.9%	17 16.7%
Says the things you want to hear	224 33.8%	36 38.6%	205 28.9%	21 20.4%
Is not serious enough	54 8.2%	10 11.1%	37 5.3%	15 14.9%
Is not emotional enough	85 12.8%	22 23.6%	80 11.3%	31 30.2%
None of these	128 19.2%	13 13.8%	134 19.0%	3 2.6%
Don't know/refused	89 13.3%	7 7.6%	141 20.0%	8 8.1%
Not having/never had sexual relations	15 2.3%	2 1.8%	34 4.7%	7 6.5%

WHAT WOMEN TALK ABOUT IN BED

So we know that men and women are dissatisfied with what they hear while making love. Now let's see what they do talk about and what they would really like to hear from their partners.

Several years ago when conducting a survey, I interviewed a number of people about what they said in bed. My survey showed that women tended to exhibit a more 'submissive' role and were mostly concerned with satisfying their mates. They seemed to have a consistent need for approval and reassurance. When I asked what they talked about with their partners when making love, some typical responses were: 'How good he felt', 'If he loved me', 'How he felt when we made love', and 'What he wanted me to do for him'.

Then I asked the women what they talked about after they made love, and found their responses to be quite different from those of men. Once again women tended to be more concerned about telling their partners how satisfied they were, how it felt, and how great their partners made them feel. These findings are parallel with those in the SEX TALK DIFFERENCES, since women tend to be more maintenance-oriented (more concerned about their mates' feelings) as opposed to task-oriented (more concerned with what they are physically doing).

WHAT WOMEN WANT
TO HEAR IN BED

Let's compare this to what women *want* to hear in bed. According to another survey I conducted for this book, fifty women and fifty men between the ages of twenty-five and sixty-two were asked what they would like to hear while making love. The women commonly responded: 'I want to hear that he loves me', 'That he thinks I'm pretty', 'That he thinks I'm beautiful', 'That I have nice breasts', 'That he likes my legs', 'That I have a nice body', 'That I make him feel good', and most of all 'That he loves me'. In essence, as confirmed by the SEX TALK DIFFERENCES, women want to be complimented. They want to hear terms of endearment and positive descriptive adjectives about themselves. They also feel more comfortable than men when receiving accolades and being praised, which translates into what is said to them during lovemaking.

Women want to be treated as individuals. This is consistent with the findings of a 1989 poll which showed that, out of three thousand women questioned, 30 per cent were annoyed at men treating them as sex objects. In essence, a man needs to express how he loves the woman on the inside as well on the outside.

Just as women have preferences regarding what they hear in bed, they also have distinct opinions on what they want to see when making love. What women do not want to look at are magazine pictures of other nude females. This was confirmed by the 1989 poll, in which 60 per cent of the women surveyed expressed this opinion. Women want to feel as though 'they' are the only woman that turns on their man, and often resent being exposed to these forms of eroticism.

If a woman finds these magazines readily accessible, she should be direct with her man and say, in a non-whining tone: 'Darling, it really makes me feel a lot better when you don't have to look at these magazines to get turned on. It makes me feel a lot sexier when you don't bring these magazines to bed with us', or 'Darling, I want to feel like I'm the only woman who turns you on.'

WHAT MEN TALK ABOUT IN BED

Men, on the other hand, answered quite differently from women. When I asked what they talked about during lovemaking, their concern seemed to centre around the 'physical aspect' of sex; they were more concerned with being in control. Some of the typical things they said in bed included: 'I'm gonna take her', 'I'm gonna fuck her', 'I'm gonna grab her and really give it to her' or 'I'm gonna screw you for hours.' These replies once again reflect the SEX TALK DIFFERENCES, as men are more task-oriented – more concerned with what they are physically doing. They also use fewer adjectives and terms of endearment, which is reflected in what they say in bed, together with stronger expletives, and swear words and slang when referring to the genitals.

I also observed that, in general, men tend to withdraw from emotional intimacy and become more detached after making love. They reported talking about food, jobs and sport at this time; this is yet another instance of the SEX TALK DIFFERENCES that men are not as emotionally open as women.

WHAT MEN WANT
TO HEAR IN BED

Compared with women, men want to hear very different things. They claim they love to hear the following comments: 'That I am the best', 'That I'm big', 'That she likes the way I make love', 'That she likes how I feel', 'That I satisfied her', 'That I make her feel good', and 'That nobody has made her feel better.' Once again these are all physical, task-oriented responses, as the SEX TALK DIFFERENCES indicate.

In the survey, when I asked the fifty men what they wanted from women during lovemaking, typical responses included: 'For women to talk more openly about what they wanted in bed', 'For women to initiate sex more often' and 'For women not to be afraid to make the first move.'

The fact that men want to hear from women that they are the 'biggest' and the 'best' may be a throwback to their childhood. Little boys are conditioned to strive to be the 'biggest' and the 'best', and to believe that nobody is better than they are. Men may want to hear these same things in adulthood. In essence, men want to hear about the physical aspect of themselves and their performance, while women want to hear how wonderful and beautiful they are and whether they are pleasing their man. Most men don't mind being a sex object in that their physical attributes are described; whereas women, as stated previously, want to be considered a 'whole person' first and foremost.

DIRTY TALK

This is another big issue about which opinions vary both between and within the sexes. Some women are completely turned off by the crudeness of 'dirty talk' during lovemaking, while others find 'dirty talk' or the use of four-letter words a sexual turn-on. Of the women I surveyed, 70 per cent found this a turn-off while only 30 per cent were turned-on.

In the other hand, 80 per cent of men enjoyed talking 'dirty', but reported that they did not like to hear it from women. This finding is consistent with the Gallup survey I commissioned for my book *Talk To Win* (Putnam, USA), which concluded that both men and women equally do not like to hear crudeness or swear words.

All this comes down to personal preference, as one of my clients, Stephanie, revealed. She might be feeling close to having an orgasm with her husband, Richard, but as soon as he started talking 'dirty' she immediately got turned off. When I asked her if she had told him how she felt, she replied that she hadn't because she didn't want to destroy the moment. I pointed out that she was destroying her own sexual moment by not communicating her desires. I suggested she say, in a very loving way, 'Darling, I know we both get very excited with each other, but it turns me on more when you say "making love", rather than "fucking" which sounds so crass and unromantic to me.' After taking my advice and telling Richard exactly how she felt, she was able to enjoy their lovemaking consistently.

If 'dirty talk' turns on both partners, there is no problem; there is only a problem when one likes it and the other doesn't. Therefore before making love you need to be open enough to ask one another whether you like to hear 'dirty talk', so that you don't inadvertently turn off your partner at a tender moment.

TEASING DURING INTIMACY

As indicated in the SEX TALK DIFFERENCES, men and women have different ways of expressing themselves where humour is concerned. Men usually regard teasing and badgering as a sign of affection, and often use it on their buddies. This locker-room humour may be fine in gyms, but it doesn't work in the bedroom. Most women don't react well to being teased about mottled thighs, small breasts, large hips or other imperfections.

One of my clients, a forty-two-year-old commodities broker, came to understand this. One morning he complained to me that he had a stiff neck from sleeping on the sofa – his wife had thrown him out of bed.

When I asked him what happened, he told me that all he had done was tease his wife about her 'bum', saying it would make a good pillow because it was so big and cushiony. He thought that was so funny – he could hardly catch his breath to control his laughter. I told him I could see perfectly well why his wife had made him sleep on the sofa. What he had said was definitely not something a woman wants to hear. Had he said it to one of his buddies, there would have been no problem; they would probably have laughed it off. But saying something like that to a woman is not funny; it is perceived as a degrading personal putdown.

Laughter is wonderful during lovemaking. In fact, having fun and communicating joy and pleasure are one of the most intimate things a couple can share. But teasing and ribbing are not acceptable to most women.

When my client finally understood he had severely hurt his wife's feelings – albeit unknowingly – by being insensitive, he realized why his wife had thrown him out of their bedroom. On the other hand, his wife didn't have to resort to such drastic measures and banish him from bed. She

111

should have been more direct and said, 'I don't find your comments about my bum very funny. In fact, it hurts my feelings that you think some part of my body is unattractive.'

Men need to understand that a woman is particularly sensitive when she is nude. A survey conducted by Steven Finch and Mary Hegarty in the July–August 1991 edition of *In Health* magazine, reported an article called 'Separating the Girls from the Boys', showed that only 22 per cent of the women liked the way they looked in the nude, while 68 per cent of men were pleased with their naked bodies. Since women in general do not have great self-esteem when it comes to their body image, it is easy to see how male 'locker-room' teasing can be misconstrued as criticism. Now that we know many of each other's preferences about what we want to hear in bed, it is up to both partners to educate one another. This is the only way to maintain a more exciting and meaningful intimate relationship.

PARTNERS ARE NOT MIND READERS

Some people think that their partner should instinctively know what their sexual desires are. Unfortunately, they are in for a big disappointment. Nobody knows what is going on inside your head unless you tell them. So you have to open up and tell your partner exactly what it is that you want sexually. Some people, however, find this embarrassing. They have not been conditioned to express their intimate needs.

According to my survey of fifty males and fifty females, close to 75 per cent of the individuals said that they felt uncomfortable expressing their innermost sexual desires and fantasies to their mate. Nearly 50 per cent of both men and women were equally uncomfortable when it came to expressing themselves openly and being 100 per cent honest and open with their partners.

Women in particular feel it is 'unladylike' to be sexually aggressive or to tell their partners exactly what they need and want. As stated in the SEX TALK DIFFERENCES, they tend to be more indirect in their communication. If a man notices that a woman is having difficulty expressing her sexual needs, he can question her gently in a soft, low tone. This technique can be used by women as well. Direct orders like 'Touch my balls' are complete turn-offs to most women. Men need to learn to use more terms of endearment, such as 'Darling, it makes me feel so good when you touch me down there.' Make requests sound gentle to the ears, and don't give harsh demands.

Tell your partner you want to learn what makes them feel good. Ask a lot of questions like: 'Does it feel good when I touch you here, or is it too sensitive?' or 'Is this too hard for you, or does it feel just right?' Also, you may want to let your partner show you how he or she wants to be touched by taking your hand and placing it over his or her body. In response, you can take your partner's hands into yours and show them what you like, and how you like things done.

If your partner is not doing something to your satisfaction, instead of saying, 'No, don't', 'Slow down' or 'Go faster' you may want to say, 'Darling, take your time' or 'Daring, I like it when you do such-and-such.' With sensitive, loving communication you become conscious of your partner's feelings and can therefore eliminate any potential misunderstandings.

INTIMACY SURVEY

To help increase intimacy in the bedroom, I designed the following questionnaire. When you and your partner fill it out you need to complete it individually – just make a copy and give one to your partner.

**My favourite romantic
fantasy is** _____

**My favourite sexual
activity is** _____

**The most sensitive parts of
my body are** _____

I love it when you _____

**If I could try one new
thing sexually it would be** _____

Touching me makes me _____

I like to be touched _____

**Talking dirty during
lovemaking is** _____

**During lovemaking I want
you to** _____

**When we kiss I love it
when you** _____

Oral sex is _____

**During intercourse I love
it when you** _____

I love it when you wear _____

My favourite scent on you is _____

114

**My favourite place to make
love with you is** _____

I don't like it when you _____

I'm not excited about _____

**I really like the following areas of my body to be caressed,
kissed or touched:**

	A lot	A little	Not at all
1. Eyes	_____	_____	_____
2. Nose	_____	_____	_____
3. Ears	_____	_____	_____
4. Lips	_____	_____	_____
5. Chin	_____	_____	_____
6. Neck	_____	_____	_____
7. Shoulders	_____	_____	_____
8. Underarms	_____	_____	_____
9. Arms	_____	_____	_____
10. Hands	_____	_____	_____
11. Fingers	_____	_____	_____
12. Breasts, upper chest	_____	_____	_____
13. Nipples	_____	_____	_____
14. Abdomen	_____	_____	_____
15. Navel	_____	_____	_____
16. Lower abdomen	_____	_____	_____
17. Genitals	_____	_____	_____
18. Thighs	_____	_____	_____
19. Buttocks	_____	_____	_____
20. Upper back	_____	_____	_____
21. Lower back	_____	_____	_____
22. Legs	_____	_____	_____
23. Feet	_____	_____	_____
24. Toes	_____	_____	_____

	A lot	**A little**	**Not at all**
25. Top of the head			
26. Forehead			
27. Hair			

FULFILLING YOUR FANTASIES

After completing your respective questionnaires, swop your answer sheets and compare notes. These answers should help promote more open conversation about what it is you enjoy. Doing the questionnaire should also allow some welcome changes and more excitement to enter your lovemaking.

If you understand each other's needs, your intimate fantasies can definitely become realities. This new shared knowledge of what you really like in bed is designed to help you increase the intimate bond between you and your partner.

TO MAKE LOVE OR NOT TO MAKE LOVE

So often couples fail to communicate their sexual desires to one another because of the fear of rejection. According to the SEX TALK DIFFERENCES, rejection is more difficult for women as they tend to personalize verbal rejection even more than men. Lovemaking is obviously the most powerful expression of intimacy that a couple can share. How often couples have sex depends on each partner's individual preferences. A good sexual relationship depends on both men and women sharing the same attitudes and having the same expectations of the sexual relationship.

According to Professor Steven W. Duck at the University of Iowa Department of Communication Studies, individuals who are emotionally sensitive tend to be more capable of expressing their desire for sex and of achieving sexual intimacy because they are more aware of their own emotional state. In other words, they are more likely to use the right approach at the right time. Similarly, their sensitivity allows them to be more aware of their partner's emotional state, which helps them to recognize when not to impose their wishes on an unwilling partner.

Let us say you initiate lovemaking, and your partner refuses you. If this is done too often and too tactlessly it can lead to a permanent communication breakdown within the relationship. But you can reject your partner's advances towards lovemaking with gentleness and sensitivity, as Anthony Pietropinto implies in his book *Not Tonight Dear – How to Reawaken Your Sexual Desire*. He suggests that you can say 'No' without rejecting your partner: you need to tell your partner why you are not interested in sex at that particular moment, and then suggest another time to make love. It is then up to you to initiate sex and make the first move next time.

If you are going to reject your partner's sexual advances, make sure you reject just the advances and not the person. Nor should sexual intimacy ever be withheld as a form of punishment. Instead, you need to communicate any dissatisfaction or problems you have with your partner so that it doesn't carry over and destroy your sex life. Women in particular, as revealed by our SEX TALK DIFFERENCES, hold grudges longer than men. So if women want to maintain good sexual relationships they need to communicate their anger and dissatisfaction openly. They also need to work on solving the problem and letting go of the anger.

INTIMATE SECRETS

When you trust another person completely you have no inhibitions about opening up and saying everything to them. You can tell them anything about your present, your past or your future. Intimately communicating means that you share your worst fears, your best thoughts, and all your innermost secrets with your partner. The more often you share your thoughts and secrets with your partner, the closer you will become. Even though there are many books that tell you not to share your innermost thoughts, I completely disagree. I feel that withholding information – a problem for many men, according to the SEX TALK DIFFERENCES – can create distance between couples, whereas sharing intimacies can only bring couples closer to one another.

However, when your partner shares an intimate secret with you it is essential never to make jokes about it and never to throw that secret back in your mate's face. This is a surefire way to destroy the relationship and break the intimate bonds forever. Men particularly need to concentrate on not using intimate information as a form of teasing to show affection: our SEX TALK DIFFERENCES show that they have a tendency to do this. But women are not immune, either.

In an intimate moment Diane shared her lifelong secret with her new husband, Eric. She told him that she had had a bulimia problem ever since she was fourteen years old and that, although she now had it under control, she did go on eating binges whenever she got extremely upset. Eric felt equally close to Diana and appreciated her candour, so shared a secret of his – that he had wet his bed until he was a teenager. A few weeks later Diane bought some new, light blue satin sheets for their bed. Thinking she was being funny, she giggled as she put the new sheets on the bed and said, 'Now, Eric, these sheets are expensive, so don't you ever wet on them!'

As she cracked up with laughter, Eric began to feel sick to his stomach. He couldn't believe what had just happened. He felt as though he had been slapped in the face and kicked in the stomach at the same time. He couldn't believe how insensitive Diane had been by throwing back at him the most intimate thing he could ever tell anyone. A wedge had been driven between the two of them, which was difficult to remove because Eric now felt that he could never share anything with Diane again. Soon he started to feel that he could no longer trust her, and eventually he found that he no longer wanted to be married to her. This unfortunate scenario is all too common. Intimate secrets thrown back into your partner's face can poison any intimate relationship forever.

INTIMATE GOSSIPING

This activity, too, can destroy a close relationship. As our SEX TALK DIFFERENCES indicate, women tend to be more open than men and to disclose more about themselves to their friends. In addition, they tend to tell secrets more often than men do, perhaps because it is something they have done since childhood. Little girls tell secrets to one another to be accepted and to develop closer bonds with their peers. Often this habit is carried over into their teens and adulthood, as women bond with other women by sharing intimate secrets.

Men don't usually do this with other men, as the SEX TALK DIFFERENCES reveal. It is not the sharing of secrets that form bonds of friendship between two boys, but physical activities. As a result, men don't sit around and gossip but joke with one another or play sports. When a women opens up and shares some intimate detail, a man doesn't understand that he is expected to reciprocate by telling a secret of his own. Women get angry and feel cheated when this doesn't happen; they are not usually aware of the sex differences in social conditioning. But as more men realize that women want them to reciprocate, they may open up and try to become more intimate.

As far as intimate secrets in general are concerned, the longer I have been in the field of communication the longer I realize that the only 'outsider' to whom you should disclose intimate problems is your doctor or therapist. Otherwise, they will usually come back to haunt you. When two people have joined forces to share a life together and to share their most intimate feelings and thoughts, what goes on in that relationship is really no one else's business.

If you are involved in an intimate relationship, and you want to maintain respect and dignity in the relationship, you need to keep the confidences of your partner at all times. Break a confidence once, and you may have destroyed a relationship forever.

LOVE IS HAVING TO SAY YOU'RE SORRY

Another SEX TALK DIFFERENCE can be seen in the way men and women apologize to one another. In the early 1970s we were all familiar with the phrase, 'Love is never having to say you're sorry', which was popularized by the movie *Love Story*. In the 1990s, if you love someone and you have a truly intimate relationship with them, 'Love is definitely having to say you are sorry.' When you love someone you have to let your partner know when you have made a mistake and how bad you feel about it. This is especially difficult for men to do, as our SEX TALK DIFFERENCES indicate. I cannot begin to recount the number of times that I have heard disgruntled clients, most often wives, say, 'If only my husband would say he was sorry and show me how terrible he feels about what happened.'

This is compounded by the fact that women do not forgive as easily as men. The word 'forgive' means basically to 'give up'. It doesn't mean to 'forget', but it does mean to 'let go'. So when women have an argument with their partner and the partner has apologized, women need to let go of their anger and not hold a grudge, as is usually the case. They must learn to accept the apology readily, especially if it is sincere.

SPEAKING THE UNSPEAKABLE

Sexual promiscuity was prevalent in past decades, but in the nineties we have to discuss some extremely intimate topics. Today, the situation regarding sexually transmitted diseases means we must be honest, open and truthful, regardless of whether we are male or female.

WHO BRINGS UP AIDS, SEXUALLY TRANSMITTED DISEASES AND SAFE SEX?

As part of the Gallup Poll I commissioned for this book, I asked 1018 men and women of eighteen and above whether they or their partner, in 'their' opinion, would be the first to bring up the topic of safe sex or getting HIV

121

tested. The question put to them was: 'At the beginning of an intimate relationship, would you be the first one to bring up the topic of safe sex and getting tested for AIDS, or do you think your partner of the opposite sex would be?'

The results showed that women (69 per cent) feel they are more likely than men (62 per cent) to be the first ones to bring up these topics. In addition, more men expected that their female partners would be the ones to bring up the topic, rather than they themselves. This result bears out the SEX TALK DIFFERENCES, which state that women confront problems more readily than men. The findings also confirm other research which shows that women tend to be more expressive and open in their relationships with men.

In a Roper Poll conducted for the US Center for Health Statistics in 1990, over eleven thousand adults were asked if they had ever discussed AIDS with a friend or a relative. In response, 64 per cent of the women stated that they had, while only 58 per cent of the men said so. The implication of this survey supports the Gallup Poll findings that women are more open when it comes to bringing up the topic of AIDS.

Gallup Poll Results – Safe Sex and Getting Tested for AIDS

	MALE	FEMALE
Total number of men and women asked	509	509
First to bring up safe sex/AIDS		
I would be	495	600
	62.2%	69.4%

	MALE	FEMALE
My partner would be	94 11.8%	52 ·6.0%
No partner/No partner of opposite sex	22 2.7%	40 4.7%
Can't say/Don't know	185 23.3%	172 19.9%

A CONVERSATION ABOUT THE UNSPEAKABLE

Since broaching the topic of AIDS can be difficult, here is an example of a conversation that may help you to be more sensitive when bringing it up:

Samantha   What are your views about getting HIV tested?

Tom   Oh, I don't think there's a problem. I don't have AIDS – I don't sleep with men.

Samantha   Well, my feeling is that everyone who has sex with a new partner should have a test.

Tom   Well, I don't think we need one – we don't have to worry about it.

Samantha   Tom, I appreciate your confidence, but I'd like to be sure. After all, if a basketball superstar like Magic Johnson can get the virus, anyone can get it. In fact I got myself HIV tested three months ago, and it came back negative. I really like you, and I'm just as concerned about your health as I am about my own. So if we're going to continue our relationship on a more intimate level, I think it's in the best interests of

123

both of us to have an AIDS test. Then we needn't have any fears.

Tom   Now that you put it that way, I tend to agree with you.

By not sounding as though she was attacking Tom, and by being honest about her own fears and yet thoughtful about Tom's health, Tom was able to pick up cues Samantha was offering which indicated not only the way she felt about him, but also the importance she attached to HIV testing. By showing her own vulnerability and tenderness, she was able to lay the groundwork for later intimacy and close communication.

TELLING YOUR PARTNER SOMETHING THEY MAY NOT WANT TO HEAR

How do you tell your partner that they have bad breath or body odour without offending them or putting them on the defensive? The key is diplomacy.

One of my clients, Tiffany, was severely upset when she came to see me recently. Apparently she had just broken up with Joshua, her boyfriend of three years. He had told her, 'You know, lately I've really not been turned on to you sexually, because you smell bad down there.'

Tiffany was devastated by his comment, as she told me that she was always conscious of her body odour and feminine hygiene. She told me that she hadn't necessarily been offended by what her boyfriend had told her, but by the way he had said it. It was so cold and blunt – which unfortunately is the *modus operandi* of too many men, as our SEX TALK DIFFERENCES indicate.

Had he said, 'Darling, you know I would never want to offend you, but I have to tell you there's an unusual odour coming from your vaginal area. Perhaps you might want to see a gynaecologist. You might have an infection or something down there, because I've never noticed it before.' Saying it in this diplomatic way would allow Tiffany not only to save face but also to escape the utter humiliation she felt because of his bluntness and insensitivity. Men need to keep this in mind.

Being a diplomat is the most important thing to consider when breaking news which the other person may not find welcoming. You have to allow them to save face and not be so embarrassed that they end up rejecting you as they remedy their problem.

Telling a person that they have bad breath also requires tact. It is often difficult to determine whether or not you have bad breath or body odour, so if a friend breaks the news they may be doing you a huge favour. But saying something like, 'Who died in here?' or 'You smell like a dead sewer rat' is obviously uncalled for, even though the 'friend' may think it is a joke. Men are more apt than women to do this kind of thing, as indicated in our SEX TALK DIFFERENCES. Sarcastic humour is not a way to break the news – diplomacy is. Instead, saying things like, 'Darling, perhaps you may have eaten something today that's affected your breath' or 'Perhaps there's something wrong with your stomach because your breath seems a little strong today. Perhaps brushing your teeth or a mouthwash might help,' are ways to allow your partner to save face. The same holds true if your partner has body odour. You need to be diplomatic by asking, for example, whether they had a particularly difficult or nerve-racking day that brought out a lot of emotional stress and perspiration. You might also suggest in a soft, loving tone that you take a bath together and relax to freshen both of you up. You can even shower together as a prelude to lovemaking.

ENDING AN INTIMATE RELATIONSHIP

Nobody likes to be rejected, and nobody likes to have to reject another person. However, when you are involved in a relationship that isn't working out you inevitably have to end it. Again, it is essential to allow the person to save face.

If you are taking the initiative, confront your partner as calmly as possible. Using the relaxation breathing techniques will often help. First, take a breath in, suck a little bit of air through your mouth, hold it for a few seconds, then slowly exhale. This can help calm you down. Second, maintain eye and face contact at all times. Third, be direct and to the point by expressing how you feel, how the relationship has affected you and what you wanted from it. Do not accuse or belittle your partner.

If someone's ending a relationship with you, try to listen. This way you may be able to learn from any mistakes you have made. Women are more apt to end a sour relationship than men. Our SEX TALK DIFFERENCES indicate that women tend to confront unpleasant situations more directly than men and are more open about their feelings. They also state that women are more likely to ask for and accept help than men, who try to work out problems on their own. Because women are on the whole more diplomatic and more open in discussing problems and in expressing how they feel, they can end relationships in a much better way than men since they know how to let their man save face.

HOW MEN CAN HAVE BETTER INTIMATE RELATIONSHIPS WITH WOMEN

1   Be more sensitive and more observant to women's non-verbal cues. For example, pay attention to how close you sit to a woman and to how much space you take up.

2   Have more facial expression and provide more non-verbal feedback, such as smiling and agreeing, as well as more head nodding.

3   Use more eye contact, especially during lovemaking. There is nothing more disconcerting for a woman than to make love with a man who does not look at her. According to surveys, most women want a man to look at her at this intimate time.

4   Become a better listener – listen to what the woman is saying and don't constantly interrupt or take over the conversation.

5   Use more tonal inflection, which women translate into more love and interest. If a man says, 'I love you', it should be spoken in a passionate tone. Don't say anything at all if you are going to say it in a boring, monotonous voice; the message can become confusing and/or misleading.

6   Be more gentle when touching and caressing; cuddle and fondle more.

7   Sloppy pronunciation such as 'comin'' or 'goin'' needs to be avoided. Women want to hear every word you say, so it is important to take your time not only during lovemaking but whenever you talk to a woman.

8 Reduce your staccato and improve your tone quality. If a man uses a very choppy tone, he will appear less approachable. Women may also perceive him as being hostile, angry or impatient. If you use a more flowing, intimate tone, the woman is more likely to be receptive to listening to you.

9 Use pitch instead of loudness for emphasis. If you need to emphasize anything, especially during an intimate moment, don't shout or say it in a loud voice. For example, use a varied pitch and put an upward inflection on the word 'love' when saying 'I love you', which gives more meaning to what you are saying. Also use a soft, rich, sexy, low voice when talking to your partner during intimacy.

10 Don't be scared to open up emotionally, especially in bed. Don't be afraid to talk about what your thoughts and feelings are, especially those that relate to your relationship with your partner. Use stream of consciousness techniques, where you let your thoughts flow and just say what is on your mind.

11 Don't use command terms, and don't ever demand. Using phrases such as 'Do this' and 'Do that' only alienate. Instead, use terms of endearment and politeness to get more positive reactions.

12 When agreeing with a woman or when acceding to her requests during lovemaking, instead of saying 'OK' or 'Yes' say 'Uhm-mmm', as this has a more sensuous sound and creates a more receptive ambiance.

13 Give more free-flowing compliments peppered with descriptive adjectives about how your woman looks, feels and smells, especially during lovemaking. Use more intensifiers and adjectives – 'You look *so* lovely', 'You look *so* incredibly beautiful', 'You feel *so* good' or 'You smell *so* terrific.'

14 Use more emotion by phrasing your comments in this way: 'I really feel . . .', 'I really wish . . .', 'I really hope . . .' or 'My feelings are . . .'. The woman will probably feel a closer bond to you; in essence you will be speaking her language. Using these phrases will help prevent alienating women.

15 Don't give minimal responses like 'Yep' or 'Nope.' Instead, draw out your tones and add phrases such as 'Yes, I would love to' or 'No, I wouldn't like to.' Open up and express yourself, not only in bed but out of bed as well.

16 Use more adjectives of adoration when speaking intimately to a woman. Studies show that women have been conditioned to want to hear how beautiful they are and how they are loved and adored.

17 Use more terms of endearment such as 'Darling', or 'Love'. These words will help bond you more closely.

18 Don't 'talk dirty' or use swear words, unless you already know that both of you are happy about this. Studies show that women in particular do not want to hear four letter words in the bedroom. To be on the safe side, you may want to find terms for body parts that you both agree upon and don't find offensive. Open communication is the answer to exploring turn-ons and turn-offs.

19 Don't be stingy with your compliments, especially during lovemaking. Just make sure you are being sincere. Don't compliment a woman on her physical attributes alone, but include her intelligence, character, warmth and compassion. And use all your senses to describe your feelings about the woman.

20 Don't ever use sarcasm to show affection, and never tease about personal or sensitive issues.

21 Don't be afraid to cry when you are feeling hurt, frustrated or angry. Many women will feel closer to you if you open up and cry in front of them, especially during highly emotional and intimate moments.

22 Don't be afraid to bring up or confront a personal issue. Don't run away from a problem. Handle it directly, honestly, openly and, of course, diplomatically.

23 Don't be afraid to bring up the topic of safe sex, sexually transmitted diseases and AIDS.

24 Don't be afraid to say you are sorry. Apologize and readily admit it when you are wrong. Use more emotion and more inflection in your tone when you apologize, so that you convey your sincerity.

25 Use softer, more sensuous tones with women, especially when you are discussing intimate aspects of your relationship.

26 Don't be afraid to ask for intimate things in your relationship. When asking for something in the bedroom the key is to use terms of endearment. Don't bark out, 'Get on top of me!' Instead, ask a question peppered with politeness and terms of endearment, such as,

'Sweetheart, why don't we try making love with you on top?'

27   When you talk to a woman in bed, you need to let the woman know that she is desirable. You need to let her know that she is sexy, feminine, wanted and desired in order for her to be more responsive to you.

28   Don't be afraid to express your emotions vocally, especially when lovemaking. Let yourself go, feel and express yourself by using genuine tones. Stifled, stilted and unexpressive tones make you sound patronizing and give women the wrong impression about you.

29   Get more detailed in your intimate communication, since women appreciate details when you talk to them. Don't just tell the bare facts.

30   Don't interrupt a woman or try to anticipate what she has to say and finish the sentence for her, especially before, during and after lovemaking.

31   While arguing or disagreeing, don't be sarcastic or joke around. Stay with the issue in question and don't change the subject; doing so creates more distance from your partner.

32   When you have to speak the unspeakable, do it with sensitivity in order not to hurt your partner's feelings.

33   If something is bothering you and a woman asks, 'What's wrong?', don't answer, 'Nothing.' Express your feelings and divulge your internal thoughts.

34   Learn to be more at ease when receiving praise and accolades about intimate aspects of yourself.

HOW WOMEN CAN HAVE BETTER INTIMATE RELATIONSHIPS WITH MEN

1   Don't expect the man to be a mind reader. Tell him what you want in a loving yet direct manner coupled with terms of endearment.

2   Don't be afraid to initiate touching your man and to make the first move sexually; surveys show that most men appreciate it.

3   Never divulge to a third party any intimate secret that a man tells you. This is a surefire way to end a relationship for good – especially if he ever finds out.

4   During lovemaking, don't be afraid to laugh and giggle. Feel free to be coquettish and playful, as this tends to put men at greater ease.

5   Don't be afraid to bring up things that you would like your partner to do for you in bed. Give him feedback concerning your immediate satisfaction by saying things like, 'You make me feel so good' or 'That's it' to let him know when you are enjoying something. This way he can keep pleasing you.

6   Don't bring up things from the past. This will be confusing and alienating, as men do not argue this way. Keep to immediate issues.

7 Let your stream of consciousness flow, especially in terms of expressing your fantasies to your mate, as this can often lead to greater intimacy.

8 Don't apologize after you confront a man about a problem. Be diplomatic, of course, but don't say you're sorry unless it is your fault.

9 Don't try to 'match' troubles with a man. If a man is sharing an intimacy with you and discussing a difficult problem, don't say that you too have a specific trouble. Instead, listen and be compassionate in order to show your support and understanding.

10 If you don't feel like making love, be diplomatic and assure your partner that it is not personal. Never withhold sex as a way of communicating your annoyance or dissatisfaction with your partner. Instead, talk about it openly.

11 Don't nag a man into opening up. Instead, let him know that you will listen should he care to talk to you about any sensitive issues. Sensitivity and tenderness often breed openness as men learn to feel safe with you.

If both men and women incorporate these guidelines into their intimate relationships, they will create for themselves not only a more meaningful union but a more sensuous and tender one as well.

6

Closing the Communication Gap at Work

From the 105 items listed in Chapter 2 there appear to be forty SEX TALK DIFFERENCES in the area of relationships with the opposite sex which, if not understood and applied, can have a shattering effect on your career. Similar SEX TALK DIFFERENCES apply to Chapters 4 and 5, but Chapter 6 will focus on different situations as it deals with male and female relationships in the workplace.

1 Men take up more physical space than women when sitting or standing; in women, this translates into a meeker presence.

2 Men gesture in a more forceful, angular and restricted manner, away from the body, with fingers pointed; women gesture in a lighter, easier, more flowing way, towards the body, with fingers apart and curved hand movements.

3 Men assume a more reclined position when sitting and listening as they lean backwards, whereas women assume a more forward position.

4 Women provide more listener feedback through body language and facial cues, and are more sensitive to non-verbal communication.

5 Men interrupt more than women when doing business.

6 Women have higher pitched voices than men. When a female voice is too high it sounds more childlike and less credible than a man's.

7 Men speak in a louder voice with more choppy, staccato tones, which often make them sound more abrupt.

8 Men use loudness to emphasize points, while women use inflection.

9 Women speak faster than men.

10 Men tend to monopolize conversations more than women.

11 Men talk more about things and activities, such as what they did and what they're going to do. Women tend to talk more about the people at work, relationships and their feelings.

12 At work, men tend to talk less about their personal lives than women.

13 Men make more direct accusations and more direct statements than women.

14 Men are less verbal and get to the point more quickly than women, who tend to beat around the bush.

15 Women tend to use more conversational lull fillers, such as 'uhm-mmm', than men.

16 Men use fewer intensifiers such as 'so', 'really' and 'quite'.

17 Men talk more about topics of conversation that they bring up, even though women raise more topics of conversation.

18 Women are more grammatically correct than men.

19 Men answer questions with a declaration, while women answer questions with another question.

20 Men make more declarative statements while women make more tentative statements – they use more tag endings and upward inflection.

21 Men make more abrupt commands, while women soften their commands with terms of politeness.

22 In business, men use fewer psychological state verbs (for example, I hope, I feel) than women.

23 Men answer questions with minimal responses, while women tend to elaborate and explain more.

24 Men use more interjections (for instance, 'Oh!', 'By the way!'), while women use more conjunctions ('and', 'but', 'however') when changing the topic.

25 Men use more qualifiers ('always', 'never', 'none'), while women use more quantifiers ('a bit', 'kind of').

26   Men make more simple requests, while women make more compound requests.

27   Men use stronger expletives and more slang words and jargon than women.

28   Men tend to lecture and to conduct more of a monologue, while women have more of a dialogue.

29   Men have a more analytical approach to problem solving, while women adopt a more emotional approach.

30   Men are more task-oriented – they will ask, 'What is everyone going to do?' Women are more maintenance-oriented and will ask, 'Is everything all right?'

31   Men use more sarcasm, practical jokes and derogatory teasing to show affection and camaraderie in the business world. They also tell more anecdotes and jokes in general.

32   Men look at things more critically and less emotionally.

33   When frustrated in business, women cry more; men tend to shout.

34   Men are more likely to impose their opinions on others than women.

35   Men are more assertive and argumentative in business.

36   Men hold grudges less than women.

37 In a business disagreement women will often bring up things from the past, while men usually stick to the immediate problem.

38 Men are less likely to ask for help and are more likely to try to work things out on their own.

39 Women tend to be more diplomatic in business, whereas men tend to be more blunt.

40 Women tend to personalize verbal rejection in the business world more than men.

For women to obtain more respect and dignity in the workforce, they need to develop more powerful and professional communication skills.

While men have been in the business world a lot longer, it is often in a woman's best interest to be more aware of the communication skills which men utilize. By understanding and incorporating many of the rules which men follow, women may enhance their own professional careers.

On the other hand, there are many lessons that men can learn from women in the business arena. It is to be hoped that, as more women learn how to communicate better at work, the ugly prejudices and sexual stereotypes will begin to disappear. Perhaps this has something to do with how women present themselves in the workforce. This chapter will not only focus on how men and women differ in their Sex Talk in the business world, but will also provide both sexes with the methods, tools and skills necessary to present themselves in a more positive and powerful way.

For obvious reasons, many of the issues in this chapter will address women.

PRESENTING THE RIGHT BUSINESS IMAGE

Often you can give the wrong impression to colleagues. This happened to a thirty-six-year-old client of mine who is a bright, beautiful, well-dressed, well-groomed invest-ment banker. She consistently increased her company's profits, yet failed to get a rise as a result. She was harassed and intimidated by her male boss, who walked all over her and treated her in a very condescending manner as though she were a child.

The problem was that, even though she looked very professional, she sounded like a schoolgirl because of her tentative, high-pitched voice. Whenever she spoke or made a statement, it appeared as though she was asking a question. It was difficult to hear her when she did speak; her voice consistently trailed off at the end of her sen-tences. Her head was often bowed down when she spoke, and her eyes looked up as though she were a shy child waiting to get scolded at any minute.

She came into my office in tears and told me what had happened to her earlier that day. It appeared that her division was about to lose a very major account, but she was somehow able to persuade the man who held this account to stay. While she was talking to her client on the phone, her boss was standing next to her listening. He wrote her a little note on a scratch pad, but it did not read 'Good job!' or 'Keep up the good work!'. Instead, it said something that shocked her: 'I can't believe you got the account back! Did you have to sleep with him?' Then he gave her a smug smirk and went back to his office. She was so angry at her boss that she took the rest of the day off and went home to sulk.

I agreed that my client's boss's behaviour was definitely wrong. However, I also pointed out that his attitude had possibly been put into motion by her own lack of communication skills. Perhaps her high-pitched voice, tentative speaking patterns, insecure body language and failure to put an end to sexist comments might all have contributed to this incident.

She agreed with me wholeheartedly, and over the next few days we worked together intensively. The following week her boss once again decided to harass and belittle her. This time she raised her head, looked directly at him, and said in a low, rich tone of voice, 'It is unacceptable to speak to me that way, and I will have none of it.' She then turned round and walked away. Her boss was stunned as she left him there with his mouth agape.

Because women have been conditioned to be unassertive, they can be easily intimidated and don't know how to communicate. In a recent survey by *Glamour* magazine it was found that, despite equal career opportunities, women felt they had fewer employment possibilities than men.

HE'S AGGRESSIVE, SHE'S A BITCH

We have seen how differently we define a person depending on what sex they are. In the business world, when a man wants something done and wants it done now he is considered to be on top of things and is regarded as an aggressive type. However, when a woman wants a colleague to act quickly and in 'her' manner, she is considered a bitch – tough and pushy.

Perhaps women are perceived as being bitchy because they use many of the male communication characteristics that are considered negative, such as speaking in harsh, non-emotional, choppy sentences. In a television interview actress Demi Moore confessed that people in Hollywood perceived her as being a bitch, when she felt she was merely being strong and opinionated. In another interview in *Vanity Fair* she added, 'If you are a woman and ask for what you want, you are treated differently than if you are a man. It's a lot more interesting to write about a bitch, than a nice woman.'

Unfortunately, these outdated stereotypes do exist. When women eliminate the female traits in their language, they sound alien or unusual to men. Men often interpret this as a negative and bitchy attitude, when in fact, it is not. When handling business situations, women do need to use masculine communication techniques; however, they can still incorporate elements of their feminine style of communication. Some of the female SEX TALK DIFFERENCES which would be helpful in the work environment are: better listening skills, making more polite requests, exhibiting warmth through facial expressions and eye contact, expressing more emotion vocally, using more psychological state verbs, and being more diplomatic. Since female communication styles are likely to encourage greater productivity than those of their male colleagues, men could well benefit from utilizing them.

In fact, Dr Judith Rosner of the University of California at Irvine has found that these feminine SEX TALK DIFFERENCES may exemplify the leadership style of the future. Women are good at inspiring others, at interacting with people, and at encouraging employees by showing them how they can reach their personal goals by participating in company-based goals.

Perhaps, as both sexes learn to incorporate the best of each other's SEX TALK DIFFERENCES in their communication styles, they can discover a more effective work relationship and create a more pleasant atmosphere on the job and in the entire business community.

BODY LANGUAGE
IN THE WORKPLACE

Men's and women's body language can be misinterpreted in a similar way. Here, too, assertive men are referred to as aggressive while assertive women are perceived as being bitches.

Whether you are male or female, if you want to be 'read' correctly and treated with more respect you need to use the right body language and body posture, as indicated by the SEX TALK DIFFERENCES. Women tend to exhibit less confident body language and head posture than men. For example, they take up less space than men, gesture more fluidly, invade another's body space less often, and lower their eyes more in negative interaction. This can often be interpreted as insecurity and lack of self-confidence. So it is essential for women to keep their heads raised and hold their shoulders back. Anthropologist David Givens at the University of Washington confirms this: he advises women at work to eliminate their 'meek cues' and appear more assertive by squaring their shoulders, not smiling as much, and leaning forward with their hands clasped in front of them on the table during meetings.

Women and men also differ with regard to their body movement and position. As shown in our list of SEX TALK DIFFERENCES, women tend to fidget less and have fewer shifts of body position. When sitting, for example, women do not move their legs and feet as often as men. They also tend to learn forward to a greater extent and to have more expressive gestures and head movements than men. This behaviour creates the illusion that women are better listeners, which can be most effective in the business world.

The occupation of space is another area of major SEX TALK DIFFERENCE. Men tend to take up more room by sprawling out or placing their arms over a chair. Also, they often spread their legs apart when they sit.

In order for a woman to look more powerful in the business world she, too, needs to take up more space. This does not, of course, mean that she has to sprawl out with her legs wide apart! It does, however, mean using plenty of room for her papers at a business meeting, or taking up more physical space at the table by spreading her arms, or gesturing away from the body when speaking. This way, a woman gives the illusion of looking more important and confident. This technique can be very effective in helping women feel as though they have a larger presence in the room, especially if they are short in stature.

One of my clients, Belinda, a five foot, seven stone aerospace engineer, told me that she felt intimidated by all her male colleagues, especially when she had to give a presentation. She simply felt dwarfed by all the large men around her.

I taught her how to feel 'bigger' by moving around the room, standing with her arms positioned on both sides of the podium, and using broad, sweeping gestures whenever she spoke. For the first time in her life, she felt more control over her audience. This in turn helped her feel more powerful and confident. Her male colleagues seemed to be more attentive and responsive throughout her presentation, too – previously, they had never been particularly good at this.

In the business arena both men and women need to look at one another as equals, especially when it comes to taking up physical space. In order to achieve a more equal status, women should never fall victim to the SEX TALK DIF-FERENCE of walking around men or moving out of their way, which conveys a feeling of submissiveness and lack of self-importance.

FACIAL IMPRESSION

Deborah Tannen's study shows that women tend to sit close and look directly at one another, while men tend to sit at angles and never to look directly at one another's face. What she is saying is that men tend to avoid eye contact by looking indirectly at one another.

It's very disconcerting not to be looked at when someone is talking to you. With this particular SEX TALK DIFFERENCE, men should learn from women to sit closer and engage in more eye contact or facial contact. But most people, of course, don't like making eye contact with another person because it makes them feel uncomfortable. Some feel threatened when directly stared at, as described in Chapter 4. Good facial contact is achieved by looking at a person's face for three seconds, at their mouth for three seconds, then at their total face again for another three seconds. Repeating this process throughout the conversation will make the other person feel you are interested in what they have to say as it is not at all intimidating.

EYE MOVEMENT

Eye movement is another very important communication style. And using the wrong movement can create misconceptions.

Thirty-three-year-old Melissa came to me to work on her communication skills. What I noticed most was that she raised her forehead and opened her eyes really wide whenever she was making a point. This made her look naïve. When I told her my observations, she wasn't surprised – one of her colleagues had told her she always looked innocent and hesitant. After learning to control her wide-eyed look, Melissa began to be treated more seriously by many of her male colleagues.

HEAD NODDING AND SMILING

The SEX TALK DIFFERENCES show that women tend to nod their heads and say 'uhm-mmm' to show agreement. While listening, women tend to smile more. But often this can be misleading, as shown by the story of Rachel and Louis.

Louis was a sales representative for a company that sold office equipment. He was trying to sell a copying machine to Rachel, an office manager. While he was giving her his sales pitch, Louis felt confident he had made a sale. Rachel kept smiling at him, looking directly into his eyes and nodding her head, giving the impression that she agreed with the reasons why her business could not profit without his product. She would constantly interject 'uhm-mmm', using an upward inflection, which was perceived by Louis as being another positive response. Louis was shocked when Rachel said she didn't want to buy a copier from him and would continue to use her old model, even though it was outdated, all the time keeping her fixed smile on her face.

Rachel's 'typically female' SEX TALK DIFFERENCE involving her facial expression gave Louis the wrong idea. Since Rachel knew all along that she wasn't going to buy the copier, she should not have allowed Louis to talk on and on and waste his time and hers. Louis was so angry at the incongruity of Rachel's cues that he never wanted to do business with her again.

145

One can easily see how Louis got the wrong impression from Rachel, who was in fact only trying to be polite and listen to what Louis had to say, as well as show interest. So in business situations it is essential for women to learn not to appear to be in agreement by nodding and saying 'uhm-mmm', unless they actually do agree. A direct approach may be best: 'I'm not interested at the present time', or 'Thank you anyway.' Facial silence may be golden in many situations. Less facial feedback, especially if you are not interested, can help the other person 'read' you a lot more easily.

In the business environment, women should smile only when it is appropriate. Unfortunately, many women smile and giggle when they are nervous. This can give the wrong impression. I am certainly not advocating that you shouldn't smile at someone and say 'Hello.' However, don't keep a smile plastered on your face all day long, especially when you are discussing serious business. Otherwise you will be sending a message that you are not serious about your work.

It should also be noted that Louis' typically male behaviour of lecturing and talking to Rachel without allowing her to get a word in edgewise contributed to their misunderstanding. Men must realize that conversation is a give-and-take proposition, like a game of tennis. A mutual back-and-forth volleying must occur, so that misunderstandings like this do not happen.

Men should also learn to provide more facial feedback when speaking to women. A study by Dr Daniel Maltz and Ruth Borker indicates that women tend to see men as cold, uninterested and intolerant when they do not provide enough facial feedback.

In summary, men need to provide women with more facial feedback when they are talking to them, while women need to limit their facial feedback to men to what is appropriate in the particular situation.

TOUCHING AT WORK CAN BE MISINTERPRETED

Touching can be perceived as leading someone on, especially if you are a woman. Candie worked for a large telecommunication firm. She was a very bright, effervescent young woman, with a great smile and personality. One day her supervisor gave her an evaluation of her progress on the job. Candie was shocked when she read the following criticism: 'You are inappropriately familiar with the clients. You touch people too much. You had better stop doing this or they may end up getting the wrong impression of you.' Embarrassing as it was to read this comment, she realized that her supervisor was right. She had been giving off the wrong impression by touching clients – her efforts at being warm and supportive were misconstrued as an open sexual invitation.

When she stopped doing this, she found that the sexual come-ons she had experienced before stopped as well. Clients now seemed to treat her with more respect. Months later, her modified behaviour helped her get the promotion she wanted.

Just as Candie became more conscious of controlling her tendency to touch, men also need to be more aware of touching women. Studies have repeatedly shown that men tend to touch women more than women touch men. Therefore, while conducting business it is in everyone's interest to keep your hands to yourself. Then no one will get the wrong impression.

'UHM-MMM' AS FEEDBACK

When women encounter men who do not provide them with verbal feedback, they conclude that the man is not listening to them. It may be in men's best interest to provide women with more feedback, not necessarily by using 'uhm-mmm' but by acknowledging what the woman is saying from time to time, or reiterating what she has said.

It is also important to monitor the frequency of your 'uhm-mmm's'. If you do it too often you will appear to be interrupting. Therefore it should be done just enough to create a give-and-take during the conversation, and no more.

IT'S NOT WHAT YOU SAY BUT HOW YOU SAY IT

It is not only what you say but the way in which you say it that can decide whether or not a person will take you seriously. You may not realize it, but speech patterns can be the major factor that determines whether a person will want to establish or continue business with you. Perhaps the greatest SEX TALK DIFFERENCES between men and women occur in how things are said. Let's look at voice patterns.

LOWERING YOUR VOICE

The example of the high-pitched 'little girl' voice given earlier is, unfortunately, an all too common SEX TALK DIFFERENCE. This voice pattern can be detrimental to anyone who wants to be taken seriously and rise up the career ladder.

Some women think that using a high-pitched voice indicates feminine charm. They are wrong – it conveys the image of an immature little girl. When I work with female clients who have this problem they soon develop a deeper, richer vocal tone and see immediate results in terms of how others treat them.

One of my clients, Debbie, had been a brilliant law student at Harvard and obtained an excellent degree. Yet despite this, she lost many job opportunities when she was interviewed by law firms because of her high-pitched voice. One male interviewer did her a big favour: he told her the truth. Even though she was embarrassed, she wasn't surprised. It was hard for people to believe that such a brilliant mind lurked under her dumb vocal façade.

In order for any woman to gain the respect she deserves and convey the proper image she must learn how to speak in a well-modulated, low-pitched voice. You can lower and deepen your voice in this way: open the back of your throat as though you are yawning, take a breath in and hold it, speak when you exhale, while keeping your teeth apart, and bear down on your stomach muscles when you speak.

Even though this is mainly a problem for women, many men experience it as well. Using the same techniques described above men can obtain a rich, resonant tone which sounds more confident and powerful.

I have helped many people in various fields to lower the pitch of their voice. One of them was actress Melanie Griffith, who starred in the film *Working Girl*. Melanie plays a secretary until one day she begins to take over the role of her boss, played by Sigourney Weaver. When Melanie imitates her boss, she consciously lowers her voice to sound more powerful and authoritative.

The pitch of your voice also helps people determine your credibility. Professor Paul Eckman at the University of California in San Francisco found that the pitch of a person's voice tends to become higher when they are lying. Other research studies have shown that individuals with higher-pitched voices are perceived to be less believable than those with lower-pitched voices. Therefore, if you want people to have more faith in you, lower the pitch of your voice – whether you are male or female.

SPEAK UP AND GET TO THE POINT

As we have seen in the previous chapters, women use more terms of endearment and politeness, have a softer way of delivering a message, and are at times not direct. Their failure to get to the point is one of the biggest complaints that men have. This is a significant issue; in the job world most people do not have time to spare. It is also important during job interviews, where answering questions succinctly can earn you the position you want. Women must learn to be more direct in order to get a foot in the door, establish confidence and literally be heard by their male colleagues.

HOW TO STOP SOMEONE INTERRUPTING YOU

Interruptions can be detrimental in the workplace if they prevent you communicating effectively. As the SEX TALK DIFFERENCES indicate, men tend to be more guilty on this account than women.

Interrupting is a most annoying habit regardless of who is doing it, as indicated in the Gallup Poll I commissioned in 1987 for *Talk To Win*. Close to 90 per cent of the people questioned felt it was the number one annoying talking habit. It can be very disconcerting, especially when doing business, as sociologists Candice West and Donald Zimmerman of the University of California at Santa Cruz have found.

Marcia, a thirty-year-old client of mine, was disturbed by the fact that her male partner consistently interrupted her. 'He's like a steam engine,' she said. 'He railroads right over me and I can't seem to get a word in edgewise. What should I do?'

I told her that, instead of having a soft, breathy voice, she needed to bear down on her stomach muscles in order to create a louder voice. And in her new, well-projected voice she needed to say, 'Please don't interrupt me, I haven't finished yet.' If her partner persisted, I told her to go on speaking over him and continue her conversation. Eventually he would get the message that she was not listening, as two people cannot talk at the same time. Marcia went home and used my technique, and the next day she was able to put an end to her partner's constant interruptions.

In order to stop a person from breaking your train of thought you need to be direct, stop the conversation immediately and use short, abrupt phrases such as 'Please don't interrupt me' or 'Let me finish first' in a loud voice.

151

Even though it worked for my client, in some instances people will be so insensitive or inattentive, and so concerned with their own agenda, that they won't even hear you telling them to stop interrupting you. If so, take a breath in, really bear down on your stomach muscles and bellow out in the loudest voice you possibly can, 'Please let me finish what I was saying!'

Perhaps one of the best responses given to a man who kept interrupting a woman was: 'Would you give me six minutes out of the sixty minutes you took to make your point?' If this still doesn't work, put your hand firmly on the other person's arm, look directly into their eyes and once again repeat, 'Please let me finish what I was saying.'

And if that doesn't work and your impulse is to punch them on the nose, you are better off leaving immediately. Just walk away, and they will get the message. But this is obviously an extreme situation, as most people are not that rude. However, if you make an interrupter aware of their bad habit on a consistent basis they will usually get the point and try to do something about it.

IF YOU ARE THE INTERRUPTER

This is one of the best ways to break the bad habit of interrupting. Before you jump in, breathe in for two seconds, hold your breath for another second, and then as you breathe out really listen to what the other person is trying to say. You won't stop interrupting overnight, but at least you will know how to control it and will therefore do so less frequently.

WATCH YOUR LANGUAGE

Robin Lakoff, who is best known for her research into female language patterns, has found that there are several things women do which make them appear to be less assertive when they talk – thus making them less powerful in the business world. According to the SEX TALK DIFFERENCES, these include the use of tag endings, ending declarative statements with an upward inflection, using emotional state verbs, and employing more adjectives and terms of endearment than men.

Tag endings are the 'questioning' bits that people add to a declarative statement, such as 'It's a thick report, *isn't it?*' This dilutes the power of the original statement and makes the speaker sound tentative and insecure. According to Robin Lakoff's study, the reason women tend to use more tag endings than men may be that they don't like to impose their views or opinions on others, as men often do.

Upward inflection makes a statement sound like a question. For example, when making a statement such as 'Get me the report' some people may inflect the word 'report' upwards, so the listener is confused as to whether or not the report is really wanted. This, too, suggests tentativeness and insecurity. More women than men are guilty of this habit, and it is in a woman's best interest to practise dropping her voice down on the last word of sentences. It will make her sound more authoritative and less like a victim.

Emotional state verbs and phrases include 'I feel', 'I'm sad', 'I hope', 'I wish' and 'I'm thrilled.' They may be useful for expressing personal information, but are not effective in the workplace. These, too, are characteristic of women's speech patterns according to Robin Lakoff. Men, on the other hand, tend to use more action state verbs and phrases such as 'I need', 'I want'. These provide more hard facts and make them sound more authoritative.

In business meetings, for instance, women will commonly ask, 'How does everyone "feel" about this issue?' In contrast, a group headed by men will often ask, 'What's the bottom line?'

Another male–female difference lies in the use of intensifiers and qualifiers. Intensifiers are words such as 'so', 'such' and 'quite', while qualifiers include 'rather', 'sort of' and 'a bit'. Women use these often; men hardly use them at all, as our SEX TALK DIFFERENCES indicate. This habit, too, makes women sound more uncertain and less forceful. To sound more powerful in their communication with men, women should exchange their qualifiers for quantifiers, such as 'all', 'none', 'always' or 'definitely', which men use. For example, instead of saying, 'These projects are usually a bit difficult' you may say, 'These projects are definitely difficult', which conveys a stronger, more firmly held opinion.

On the other hand, men would benefit from incorporating more qualifiers, especially when offering criticism and expressing differences of opinion. Qualifiers will help them sound more approachable and less abrupt.

Adjectives, of course, qualify nouns. Studies indicate that women use them most often when expressing admiration, when they use words such as 'adorable', 'charming' and 'sweet'. Although the use of adjectives may be a good thing in one's personal life, in business it is the bottom line that counts.

One of my male colleagues once told me about a female business associate who embarrassed him whenever they saw a client together. She would say, 'Oh, isn't this a lovely office?', 'What a sweet thing to do!' or 'Look at that adorable man.' He found her statements unprofessional, and subsequently weakened their effectiveness as a business team.

Women need to limit these typical female language patterns when communicating with men. However, men need to make an effort at better communication, too. They should, for instance, use more emotional state verbs and say they 'feel good' about a project or are 'thrilled' or 'ecstatic' about what happened, or are extremely 'distressed' about the situation. Also, they should replace some quantifiers with qualifiers to soften their statements when appropriate. In this way men and women can learn from one another's SEX TALK DIFFERENCES, which will enhance and improve communication in the workplace.

EVERYONE NEEDS POLITENESS AT WORK

Using terms of politeness is one of the most significant communication techniques that men can learn from women. Men will often use command terms like 'Get me a file' or 'Let's get to the bottom line' rather than terms of politeness like 'Would you mind getting me the file.' Barking out commands is completely unacceptable in business. Politeness and kindness can combat rudeness in general and can win support from either sex. This was clearly illustrated in the 1990 election campaign for Governor of Texas, a race fought between Ann Richards and Clayton Williams. During this rather ugly, dirty political campaign, Williams went up to Richards at a luncheon and called her a liar. This was set to turn into a media event. But instead of retaliating with a similar comment Ann Richards remained dignified, looked directly at her rival and said, in a calm, direct voice, 'Clayton, I'm sorry you feel that way.' Her response to this incident may have helped her win the election.

DON'T APOLOGIZE
UNLESS IT'S YOUR FAULT

To appear polite, women will often apologize by saying, 'I'm sorry' or 'I didn't mean to'. Deborah Tannen confirms that women tend to apologize too often, even when they don't need to. Certainly it is fine to say 'I'm sorry' when you have made a mistake or are out of line, but it is definitely inappropriate to do so when you are not.

Men find this behaviour very confusing, especially when you apologize for something you have not done or for speaking your mind or losing your cool. You diffuse your power and reduce your credibility. In essence, you come across as being indirect, unstable and wishy-washy.

Instead of saying, 'I'm sorry I raised my voice', just say, 'I know I raised my voice, but I was very irritated. Things got to that point because you didn't hear what I was trying to say.' Instead of saying, 'I'm sorry for saying what I said', you need to say, 'I said it because I meant it, and even though it may have hurt your feelings I had to be completely honest with you.'

Confronting someone directly is not a mistake. Just be polite. If you talk in a tone that is gentle and positive, yet firm, you can get your message across more effectively.

KEEPING YOUR PERSONAL
LIFE PERSONAL

According to surveys, women tend to disclose details of their personal lives at work. They talk about their husbands, relationships, children and feelings about other people. Men, on the other hand, rarely discuss these things. Revealing personal information can often come back to haunt you: you can lose professional credibility and respect.

This happened to a client of mine who shared a problem in her personal life with several of her male and female colleagues. While having coffee one morning, she told them she really wanted to divorce her husband because he came home drunk all the time. She went on and on about his irresponsibility and how he constantly upset her.

A few weeks later, one of her colleagues said jokingly, 'How's that drunken bum of yours?' My client flushed with embarrassment, as the situation between her and her husband had improved greatly. Later that week another male colleague, after discovering several errors in her data, snidely commented, 'Maybe that good-for-nothing husband of yours is keeping you up all night so you can't concentrate on your work.' My client certainly learned her lesson the hard way: to keep her personal life just that – personal.

DON'T FLIRT
UNLESS YOU MEAN IT

No book of this nature could be complete without a section on how to deal with sexist comments. Even though men reportedly experience sexual harassment from women, historically it has been common for women to face this problem in the workplace. In the 1990s it is time that we put an end to any form of sexual harassment, regardless of gender.

One of my clients, Rafael, a very good-looking journalist, was fired because he did not respond to the sexual advances of his female boss. But when I asked him to go over the situation with me in detail, I found that he had actually encouraged her flirtations.

Rafael's boss was a woman to whom he was not attracted. However, he was happy in his job and wanted to keep it. So he encouraged her, and flirted right back at her. This obviously gave his boss the wrong impression: she thought he liked her, too. He thought nothing of accepting her dinner invitation, but became appalled when she began to 'get physical'. When Rafael said goodbye to her advances, he also had to say goodbye to his job; it was too embarrassing for his boss to keep him around.

Even though this scenario is not as common with men as it is with women, it does bring up a very important point – that you are responsible for your own flirtations. In most cases flirting is fun, innocent and harmless. However, if you want to remain professional at work it is important to cheek a check on your behaviour. If you are going to flirt in the workplace, make sure your intentions are sincere and that the person you are flirting with cannot harm you professionally. This is in case either of you should lose your attraction towards the other.

DON'T CALL ME 'SWEETHEART'

Terms of endearment are wonderful to hear in the bedroom, but not in the board room. When used by men to women in the business world, they can take an entirely different meaning and in fact be perceived as pejorative. One morning I heard the regular doctor on a TV show call the female co-host 'sweetheart'. A fleeting thought went through my mind: were they having an affair or were they just good friends? When he had finished his report I heard his co-host say, 'OK, honey' – at which he seemed visibly taken aback. She immediately interjected in an annoyed tone, 'You called me, sweetheart, right before you did your piece.' One might think: 'What's the big deal? So what if he called her sweetheart. He was just being friendly.' But he did not treat his colleague with the professional respect she deserved, and she let him know it.

Women have come a long way in terms of how they are referred to by men. In 1984 a *Newsweek* study asked whether women were bothered when men referred to them as 'girls'. Only 34 per cent reported that they were annoyed, while 51 per cent stated that it didn't bother them at all. However, five years later another survey showed that 53 per cent of women were annoyed, while only 44 per cent were not. More women now considered that being referred to as a 'girl' was disrespectful and sexist.

One of the fastest ways for men to alienate women at work is by calling them 'girls', as a doctor I once knew did. He not only referred to his secretarial staff as 'girls' but used the term for his female professional colleagues as well. He was quite unaware of the effect he was having and could not understand why his office staff always seemed to sabotage his requests. Nor could he work out why so many of the women doctors whom he knew were abrupt, impatient and intolerant with him. It wasn't until one of these colleagues said, 'Look, stop calling me a "girl". A "girl" is not a doctor – a woman is. I'm your equal – your colleague – so please show me the same respect that I show you.' After making a conscious effort to stop using the term he started to notice how much more work his secretary and his female staff were doing for him, and how much more cooperation he was receiving from his female colleagues.

In essence, men need to become aware of how seemingly innocent terms, 'labels' and terms of endearment may be perceived as sexist.

HANDLING SEXUAL COMMENTS

Unfortunately, this evolved awareness has not penetrated every working environment. Verbal sexism is still quite prevalent in areas like the police, according to a recent report on the Los Angeles Police Department.

It showed that women were discriminated against and trivialized. According to SEX TALK DIFFERENCES, some men think nothing of using swear words, four letter words, verbal jabs or barbs as a form of teasing to show they accept the other person. This does not go down very well with women. It was found that on computer screens women in the police force were being called 'sweetcakes', 'babes', 'Barbie Dolls', 'Sergeant Tits' and 'cunts'. According to the report, some women officers testified that computer messages such as 'Get a job, woman, one that is more suited for a woman, such as a secretary or a receptionist' or 'Don't give me any lip, woman, just obey' left the women officers feeling personally insulted and professionally undercut – even though they were intended to be humorous. Most women officers who were interviewed by the Police Commission said they tended to shrug off such messages as inconsequential banter, regarding them as the release of tension experienced by male police officers.

Unfortunately, all too many men are still dinosaurs. Since they have not changed with the times, they need to be told immediately and directly by women that their behaviour is unacceptable and not funny, as Linda Putz of the Los Angeles Police Department revealed in the *Los Angeles Times*: 'Most of the times, I am not thin-skinned, I don't think most of the people on the job are. I can tease anybody just as they can tease me. But once in a blue moon, I have to tell somebody I don't like that, and they stop.' The key is to confront and reject sexist comments immediately, letting the man know that he has over-stepped his bounds.

JUST JOKING

As mentioned in the previous section, the SEX TALK DIFFERENCES indicate that most men find humour in needling and harassing employees and male bosses. Men tend to show affection towards their staff by teasing them; however, most women are offended by this. Unlike men, women tend to personalize these comments.

Men need to realize that women do have a sense of humour, but they do not like to be the brunt of the joke. On the other hand, as women become more aware of the disparity in perception of humour between the sexes they need to realize that humour which they may find offensive may merely be a display of acceptance towards them. Therefore women should learn to avoid personalizing many of their male colleagues' remarks. Sexist or offensive jokes should simply not be acknowledged. Ignoring them can often be the best way to condition a man to stop making these negative remarks. If a man repeatedly gets no response – not even a wince – they will usually stop.

However, there are times when a woman definitely needs to respond, especially if she feels personally insulted by the comment. She should say, 'I'm sure you didn't mean to insult me, but I find your comment most offensive', or 'Is there any reason why you particularly want to hurt my feelings by saying something like this?', or 'Are you aware of how very disrespectful to me your remark is?' By acknowledging the remark and confronting it directly, openly and honestly, the woman is setting the limits by letting the man know that there are certain comments that are unacceptable. This reaction will put a stop to such offensiveness.

WHEN WOMEN CRITICIZE MEN

When a woman criticizes a man at work, she needs to be objective and to the point and not over-polite. Otherwise the message gets lost or is at best diluted.

Ralph's boss, Jane, kept telling him over and over again that his report was not presented in the way she wanted it. The seventh time she handed him back the report she was so angry that she said bluntly, 'Ralph, this is not the way I want it. Take out this section, leave this one in, and put this section at the end.'

Ralph who was also upset after going back and forth with Jane, replied, 'Why didn't you tell me exactly what you wanted in the first place?'

Jane thought she made herself clear, but obviously she had not. She realized that she might have been too considerate, vague and soft-spoken, so Ralph did not understand what she was trying to get across. When she was more direct and to the point, he definitely heard the message.

WHEN MEN CRITICIZE WOMEN

On the other hand, when men criticize women they need to be concerned not only about what they say but about how they say it. They should incorporate more terms of politeness and should phrase criticisms in a positive rather than a negative way. Asking, 'Don't you think it could be more effective if you did so-and-so?' or saying 'I know you've done a very good job on this project. However, it may not be the best idea to do such-and-such,' will be better received by women than 'I don't like this.' Using more emotional state verbs in order to make the message more palatable ('I feel that it might be a better idea . . .' or 'I'm unhappy about . . .') shows more sensitivity when expressing critical comments to a woman. Using these positive and diplomatic approaches not only takes the edge off the criticism but allows for the woman to save face.

CRYING AT WORK

For the most part, crying is a no-no in the business world; but there are times when it is acceptable, such as when one is sentimentally touched or emotionally moved. After all, General Norman Schwarzkopf wept when he relinquished his command after the Gulf War. He was reported as having wiped tears from his eyes several times during his farewell speech. His honest, open display of emotion may have further endeared General Schwarzkopf to those Americans who supported him.

However, tears can be the death knell when they are used to release anger or frustration in the workplace. One of my clients, Judith, found this out. Because she had not made enough sales she was being criticized by her boss, who shouted loudly and angrily at her in front of her colleagues. Instead of saying with confidence, 'You have no right to shout and talk to me like this, especially in front of my colleagues', Judith was so intimidated by her boss's volcanic sound that she began to cry right in front of everyone. From that time forward, her boss knew he could use her as his whipping post. She lost her prominence in her department and never regained it.

Women, in particular, need to gain more control over tears. For the most part they tend to cry in order to fend off criticism, to dispel tension or to express anger. Men, on the other hand, frequently release tension or express anger by swearing and shouting. It is a way of coping that has been conditioned into them since childhood, as we explained in Chapter 3. Neither display of emotion is very effective in the business world. In fact it is the cool, controlled individual who is treated with more professional respect.

If you feel like crying, try to bite your lips, slap or pinch yourself until you find a safe and private place to let out your emotions. There is truth behind the old axiom: if you need to cry, do it behind closed doors.

I once knew a male newscaster whose eyes welled up with tears while reading a story about a young child who had been brutally killed. It took all the self-control he could muster to keep the tears from rolling down his cheeks. As soon as they switched to a commercial he broke down. Being the professional he was, he had managed to hold himself together while he was on camera. But being the man he was, he was able to let himself go when it was safe to do so.

YOU CAN'T AFFORD TO HOLD A GRUDGE AT WORK

Karen, an executive in a large advertising firm, came into my office perplexed. She and two male colleagues, Steve and Gary, had been assigned to work on a particular project. Karen stayed up all night preparing a proposal which she thought was terrific. She felt it was truly a stroke of genius which represented the creativity and freshness that the client was looking for.

The next morning she presented her proposal to her two male partners. Gary thought it was the most ridiculous thing he ever heard. Steve, on the other hand, thought it was wonderful. In order for the project to be successful all three had to agree, and this was obviously not going to happen. Some severe language resulted, and a big argument. Karen passionately and aggressively defended her ideas and became angrier and angrier with Gary. She called him stubborn, ignorant and uncreative.

Steve saw Karen's viewpoint and defended her with equal vigour. After three hours of going back and forth and not getting anywhere, Steve suggested that they should all go out to lunch. Karen was stunned and could not believe that Steve had actually suggested their doing this when she was so angry. She refused to go out, ordered a sandwich and ate alone in her office.

As she looked out of the window she could see Gary and Steve walking down the street to the restaurant. They were joking with one another, laughing and having a good time, as though nothing had happened. Karen was still fuming. She could not understand how Steve could be so friendly to Gary when they had almost come to blows in the conference room.

This example clearly illustrates how differently men and women handle arguments and disagreements in the workplace. Men tend to look at them as contests with a beginning, middle and end, but women are not conditioned to see arguments in this light. They tend to personalize them and to harbour negative feelings towards their opponent – they bear a grudge. In the business world there is little room for grudges or ill feelings; the key is professionalism at all times. There is nothing wrong with 'lunching with the enemy', as in Karen and Gary's case. Their disagreement was professional, not personal.

Perhaps men see losing an argument and not harbouring ill feelings as good sportsmanship, which they learn as small boys when they play sports and their team loses. As youngsters they are taught that being a good sport is just as important as winning the game. The boys still remain buddies with the other team and only look at their opponents as adversaries during the game. Most women, on the other hand, are not conditioned to do this. They do not have as many team experiences as boys. As a result, when they grow up and enter the business world they may not be sensitive to 'good sportsmanship'.

In order to create more productive, cohesive and businesslike relationships women need to let go of all animosity and continue being professional when doing business with their adversaries. They must become more objective about their work.

WHAT WOMEN NEED TO DO WHEN WORKING WITH MEN

1 Don't minimize your accomplishments at work. If you have done something that you're proud of, don't be afraid to express it. Men are conditioned to proclaim they are the greatest at certain things. Don't be afraid to follow suit.

2 Never discuss anything personal at work. Instead, talk about job-related issues, news events and even sports, as these are topics that most men can relate to.

3 When you talk with male colleagues, discuss what you did, where you are going and where you went, but not how you feel. Be more objective and less emotional. Instead of using words such as 'I think', 'I feel' and 'I hope', make direct statements such as 'It is', 'We will', and 'There are'.

4 In business meetings, try to take up more space and sit in a more relaxed position. Do not hesitate to spread out your papers.

5 Use larger, sweeping gestures to convey more self-confidence.

6 When you are speaking to a room full of people, don't stay in one place. Instead, walk around. This will give you a more powerful presence.

7 Lower the pitch of your voice to sound like an intelligent professional woman. High-pitched voices sound less credible and more childlike.

8 Don't talk quickly and don't be a chatterbox. Slow down. Take your time when pronouncing sounds, drawing out your syllables so that every word you say can be understood. Remember, every sound you make is important.

9 Get to the point. Your primary statement should include who, what, when, where and how. Then, if you need to elaborate, enumerate the points you wish to discuss. First, tell people that you will discuss certain issues in a certain order. Then follow a logical progression from point to point as you explain yourself, which makes it clearer to the listener.

10 Speak up, and don't let any man get away with interrupting you. If someone doesn't let you get a word in edgewise, speak over him. If he persists, continue to increase the volume of your tone so that he becomes aware that his interruptions are unacceptable.

11 Don't use 'tag endings', such as 'This is a difficult report, *isn't it?*' They make you seem unsure of yourself.

12 Don't answer a question with another apparent question. If someone asks you the time, for example, don't use an upward inflection and say, 'It's two o'clock?' Rather, drop your tone to make a declarative statement.

13 When changing topics, use interjections or exclamatory words instead of conjunctions like 'and' or 'but'. Don't say, 'And I think such-and-such.' Say, 'Well, it appears to be such-and-such.'

14 Use stronger quantifiers, like 'always', 'none' and 'never', and fewer qualifiers, like 'kind of' and 'a bit'. Quantifiers will make you sound more confident and factual, and less tentative.

15 Make a number of simple requests instead of one long, complex one – make one request, then another, and so on. Convoluted requests lose their potency.

16 Learn work-related slang or jargon and use it when talking to male colleagues.

17 Don't be offended by sarcastic comments or practical jokes. Realize that this is a form of male bonding.

18 On the other hand, if you feel like teasing and practical jokes are out of line (for example, if they are sexist or extremely offensive) be open and direct and immediately let the man know he has overstepped his bounds. Don't let your anger fester.

19 Look at situations and events in the workplace more critically and objectively and less emotionally.

20   When criticizing a male employee, be direct and to the point. Don't dilute what you are saying with so much politeness that the message gets lost.

21   Whatever you do, don't cry in front of others. If you must cry, do so in private. Otherwise you may lose your professional credibility.

22   Try to ignore men when they swear, and don't take it personally. Not responding will often put an end to it. Don't chastise or reprimand. However, if the swearing is directed at you put a stop to it by using a firm tone and letting the man know his behaviour is unacceptable.

23   You don't have to use swear words to be one of the guys.

24   If you have a major disagreement with a colleague, maintain your professionalism and don't hold a grudge. Remain cordial, even lunching with the enemy if necessary.

25   Try to tell some anecdotes and jokes to lighten up the mood and to show that you too have a sense of humour. The stories don't have to be crude, vulgar, sexist or racist, but they can be anecdotal. Your colleagues might find them humorous, which in turn will create more common ground between you and them.

26   Be conscious of how often you nod your head and smile. Try to keep this body language at a minimum during business interactions. If not, you may miscommunicate how you really feel about a situation.

27   Don't apologize unless you are wrong. Stop saying, 'I'm sorry' just to be polite.

28 When you are excited, don't open your eyes wide when you speak. This gives the illusion of innocence and tentativeness, a facial gesture that may not elicit trust from male colleagues.

29 Don't personalize verbal rejection. Instead, be objective and businesslike about the situation.

WHAT MEN NEED TO DO WHEN WORKING WITH WOMEN

1 Be considerate and don't use swear words when women are around.

2 The same holds true for sexist jokes and comments. This type of humour has no business in the workplace.

3 Use more terms of politeness when speaking to women. Don't forget the key words 'Please' and 'Thank you'.

4 Don't bark out commands or orders when talking to women. Instead, make more polite requests.

5 Don't be afraid to ask for help. The sooner you ask for assistance, the quicker you will receive it and accomplish what you have to do. Forget about your ego.

6 Don't shout or swear to release frustration at work. Instead control your temper and handle yourself in a professional manner at all times.

7 Provide more facial and verbal feedback when talking with women.

8 Don't address women as 'honey', 'dear', 'babe' or 'sweetheart'. Nor should you refer to them as 'girls'. All may be misinterpreted as chauvinistic and condescending.

9 Don't interrupt or monopolize conversations, and never speak for a woman.

10 Make more direct facial contact. Look directly at the woman you are speaking to, and not from an angle or off to the side. Not making direct, facial contact gives a woman the impression that you are not giving her your full attention, or that you don't consider what she has to say is important.

7

Closing
the Communication Gap
for Good

Who is your best friend? Is your best friend a man or a woman? This is a question that was asked in a recent Gallup Poll of 911 adults. Almost 70 per cent of the men said that their best friend was a man, while only 18 per cent said it was a woman. Eighty per cent of the women surveyed reported that their best friend was a woman, and 20 per cent said it was a man.

Based on what we have seen throughout this book, it is no wonder that, when it comes to friendships which involve opening up and sharing experiences and feelings, men tend to seek out other men and women to seek out other women. Perhaps the reason is that up until now women have not understood how to talk to men, and conversely men have not understood how to talk to women.

Shere Hite's findings in her book *Woman and Love, A Cultural Revolution in Progress* confirm the results of this Gallup Poll. Close to 90 per cent of the married women she surveyed stated that they had their deepest relationship with a woman friend as opposed to having this relationship with their husband. Once again, it is probable that their response had something to do with the fact that men and women do not know how to communicate with one another.

The only way we can ever close the communication gap between one another is if men and women learn to become each other's best friends. This means understanding each other's needs.

Previously we really did not understand the differences between men and women, or how they affected our personal, intimate and business relationships. Now that we know what to do, what to say and how to say it, there is no excuse for miscommunication between men and women.

HUMAN TRAITS, NOT GENDER-SPECIFIC TRAITS

In Ashley Montagu's book *The Natural Superiority of Women* he mentions that there are several traits which men have deemed feminine, such as gentleness, tenderness and loving kindness. He states that these are not just feminine traits, but rather 'human traits which men need to adopt and develop if they are ever to be returned to a semblance of humanity'. Unfortunately, with regard to the differences between men and women we accept far too many stereotypes that are outdated, outmoded and incorrect.

Both men and women once knew what their stereotyped roles were and dared not deviate. But we no longer live in a world where the mother's place was in the home and the father went to work and everyone lived happily ever after.

In the Western world the past twenty years have been flooded with changing views on how men and women are perceived. In a 1970 US study a group of psychologists asked almost eighty male and female therapists to define what characteristics they felt constituted a 'mentally healthy male' and a 'mentally healthy female'. The male was considered to have the following attributes: aggressiveness, independence, objectivity and autonomy. The female, on the other hand, was defined as submissive, dependent and subjective. We've certainly come a long way in terms of what constitutes a mentally healthy male or female by today's standards. Perhaps a mentally healthy person of today would share 'all these traits' which are 'human-specific characteristics', as Ashley Montagu indicates, rather than 'gender-specific'.

Even though we've come a long way, our past conditioning and socialization has created many problems for both men and women. There is nothing particularly wrong with the fact that men are different from women, and that they communicate differently. The problem arises when men and women have so much tension and turmoil between them that they become insensitive to one another's needs.

In the 1990s not knowing how to communicate with the opposite sex is so serious an issue that it can cost you your livelihood as well as your personal happiness. In today's world, you have no choice but to learn the SEX TALK RULES that will once and for all get rid of the pain and aggravation that miscommunication can create.

The only way we can ever win the battle of the sexes and close the communication gap forever is through awareness, understanding and compromise. Men and women are not adversaries or opponents. We are all on the same team.

Men and women harbour the same fears, wants and needs. We are all afraid of rejection and alienation. We all want to be loved, respected and admired. It is only through open and honest communication with one another that we can make our lives fuller and richer. Only by doing this can we have a more peaceful coexistence between the sexes.

The information in this book will help you deal with all those annoying differences which create potential problems among loving couples as well as business associates. Whenever you find yourself having problems communicating with the opposite sex, do not hesitate to reread this book. Each time you will gain more new insights, which can then be incorporated into your existing relationships as well as new ones. In the process you might even gain further insight into yourself as well.

WHERE TO GET
MORE INFORMATION

If you wish to receive more personalized information please send this page with a SELF-ADDRESSED envelope and an international response coupon to:

**Dr Lillian Glass
c/o Your Total Image Inc.,
435 N. Bedford Drive, Suite 209
Beverly Hills, CA 90210. USA
or call 0101 (310) 274 0528**

Name: ....

Address: ....

Post Code, Country: ....

Phone Number (and area code): ....

Please send me information on the following:

.... Additional Books by Dr Glass

.... Audiotapes

.... Videotapes

.... Workshops and Group Seminars in Your City

.... Lectures to Companies

Where to Get More Information

.... Personal Telephone Evaluations with Dr Glass

.... Audiotape Evaluation of Your Communication
          Skills

.... Private Sessions with Dr Glass

.... Communication Skill Improvement

.... Voice Therapy

.... Stuttering Therapy

.... Speech and Language Therapy

.... Voice Improvement

.... Telephone Evaluation of Your Voice

.... Video or Audiotape Evaluation

.... Newsletter

.... Accent or Dialect Reduction or Instruction

Source List

Abbey, Antonia. 'Sex Differences in Attributions for Friendly Behavior – Do Males Misperceive Female Friendliness?' *Journal of Personality and Social Psychology* 5 (1982): pages 830–38.

Allen, Laura S. and Roger A. Gorski. 'Sex Difference in the Bed Nucleus of the Stria Terminalis of the Human Brain.' *The Journal of Comparative Neurology* (1990): pages 302–667.

Applegate, Jane. 'Women–Male Domination is Fading.' *Los Angeles Times* (July 1991): B1.

Associated Press. 'Schwarzkopf Weeps as He Relinquishes His Command.' *Los Angeles Times* (10 August 1991): A20.

Bailey, Patricia. 'Television Cartoons Perpetuate Stereotypes.' *University of California, Berkeley Clip Sheet* (6 August 1985): page 1.

Barbach, Lonnie and Linda Levine. *Shared Intimacies*. New York: Doubleday, 1980.

Barbach, Lonnie. 'Talking in Bed – Now That We Know What We Want – How Do We Say It?' *Ms* (January 1991): pages 64, 65, 80.

Best, Raphaela. *We've All Got Scars – What Boys and Girls Learn in Elementary School*. Indiana: Indiana University Press, 1983.

Beyer, Lisa. 'Life Behind the Veil.' *Time* (Fall 1990): page 37.

Birdwhistell, Raymond. 'Masculinity and Femininity as Display', in *Kinesics and Context*. Philadelphia: University of Pennsylvania Press, 1970: pages 39–46.

Bornoff, Nicholas. *Pink Samurai: Love, Marriage and Sex in Contemporary Japan*. New York: Pocket Books, 1991.

Brecher, John and James Pringle, Carl Robinson, Douglas Stanglin. 'Low Blow Down Under.' *Newsweek* (18 May 1981): page 71.

Brend, Ruth. 'Male–Female Intonation Patterns in American English', in *Language and Sex: Difference and Dominance*. Edited by Barrie Thorne and Nancy Henley. Rowley, Massachusetts: Newbury House, 1975.

Brodermen, D. M. and F. E. Clarkson, P. S. Rosenkrantz, S. R. Vogel. 'Sex Roles Stereotypes and Clinical Judgements of Mental Health.' *Journal of Consulting and Clinical Psychology* 34 (1970): pages 1–7.

Bumiller, Elizabeth. 'Love, Japanese Style.' *Los Angeles Times* (22 September 1991): page 4.

Burton, Sandra. 'Condolences: It's a Girl.' *Time* (Fall 1990): page 36.

Cantor, Joanne R. 'What's Funny to Whom.' *Journal of Communication* 26 (1976): pages 164–72.

Carlson, Margaret. 'Is This What Feminism Is All About?' *Time* (24 June 1991): page 57.

Collins, Glenn. 'Language and Sex Stereotypes.' *This World* (26 April 1981): page 23.

Coleman, Ron. 'A Comparison of the Contributions of Two Voice Quality Characteristics to the Perception of Maleness and Femaleness in the Voice.' *Journal of Speech and Hearing Research* 19 (1976): pages 168–80.

Coleman, Ron. 'Male and Female Voice Quality and Its Relationship to Vowel Formant Frequencies.' *Journal of Speech and Hearing Research* 14 (1971): pages 120–25.

Collins, Nancy. 'Demi's Big Moment.' *Vanity Fair* S4, No. 8 (August 1991): pages 96–102.

Collins, Eliza G. C. 'Managers and Lovers.' *Harvard Business Review* (September/October 1983): pages 142–53.

Dion, Kenneth L. and Regina A. Schuller. 'Ms. and the Manager: A Tale of Two Stereotypes.' *Sex Roles* 22, no. 9/10 (May 1990): pages 569–78.

Dolnick, Edward. 'Superwoman.' *In Health* (July/August 1991): pages 42–3.

Dorman, Lesley. 'Doesn't Every Woman Have Her Own Ideas About What Makes a Man Great in Bed?' *New Woman* (March 1991): pages 48–50.

Dullea, Georgia. 'Relationships, the Sexes, Differences in Speech.' *New York Times* (19 March 1984): A1.

Eakins, Barbara Westbrook and R. Gene Eakins. *Sex Differences in Communication*. Boston: Houghton Mifflin, 1973.

Eaton, William J. and Norman Kempster. 'Senators Want Glaspie Issue Clarified.' *Los Angeles Times* (13 July 1991): A3, A9, A10.

Edelsky, Carole. 'Acquisition of an Aspect of Communicative Competence: Learning What It Means to Talk Like a Lady.' *Child Discourse*. Edited by S. Ervin and C. Mitchell-Kernan. New York: Academic Press, 1977.

Edelsky, Carole. 'Question Intonation and Sex Roles.' *Language of Sociology* 8 (1979): pages 15–32.

Ellis, Barnes C. 'Back Off to Avoid Sexual Harassment Bogle Warns.' *The Oregonian* (19 March 1991): B1.

Fagot, B. I. 'Consequences of Moderate Cross-Gender Behavior in Preschool Children.' *Child Development* 48 (1977): pages 902–7.

Farb, Peter. *Word-Play: What Happens When People Talk*. New York: Alfred A. Knopf, 1973.

Feinman, Steven. 'Approval of Cross-Sex-Role Behavior.' *Psychological Reports* 35 (1974): pages 643–8.

Feinman, Steven. 'Why is Cross-Sex-Role Behavior More Approved for Girls than for Boys? A Status Characteristic Approach.' *Sex Roles* 7 (1981): pages 239–99.

Finch, Steven and Mary Hegarty. 'Separating the Girls from the Boys.' *In Health* (July/August 1991): page 48.

Frieze, Irene Hanson and Sheila J. Ramsey. 'Non-verbal Maintenance of Traditional Sex Roles.' *Journal of Social Issues* 32, no. 3 (1976): pages 133–41.

Furnham, Adrian and Catherine Hester, Catherine Weir. 'Sex Differences in the Preferences for Specific Female Body Shapes.' *Sex Roles* 22, no. 11/12 (June 1990): pages 743–54.

Garcia-Zarmon, Marie A. 'Child Awareness of Sex Role Distinctions in Language Use.' Paper presented at Linguistics Society of America, December 1973.

Gerai, Joseph E. and Amram Scheinfeld. 'Sex Differences in Mental and Behavioral Traits.' *Genetic Psychology Monograph* 77 (1961): pages 169–299.

Gelman, David and John Carey, Eric Gelman, Phyllis Malamud, Donna Foote, Gerald C. Lubenau, Joe Contreras. 'Just How the Sexes Differ.' *Newsweek* (28 May 1981): pages 71–83.

Gelman, David and John Carey. 'Sex Research – On the Bias.' *Newsweek* (18 May 1981): page 81.

Gilligan, Carol. *In a Different Voice: Psychological Theory and Women's Development*. Cambridge, Massachusetts: Harvard University Press, 1982.

Givens, David. 'You Animal.' *Success* (1987): pages 50–53.

Glass, Lillian. *Confident Conversation: How to Talk in Any Business or Social Situation*. London: Piatkus, 1991.

Glass, Lillian. *Talk to Win – Six Steps to a Successful Vocal Image*. New York: Perigee Books–Putnam, 1987.

Gleason, Jean Berko. 'Code Switching in Children's Language,' in *Cognitive Development and the Acquisition of Language*. Edited by Timothy E. Moore. New York: Academic Press, 1973: pages 159–67.

Gleason, Jean Berko and Esther Blank Greif. *Men's Speech to Young Children in Language Gender Society*. Edited by Barrie Thorne, Cheris Kramar and Nancy Henley. Rowley, Massachusetts: Newbury House, 1988: pages 140–50.

Gleason, Jean Berko. 'Sex Difference in Parent–Child Interaction,' in *Language and Gender and Sex in Comparative Perspective*. Edited by Susan U. Philips, Susan Steele and Christine Tanz. Cambridge: Cambridge University Press, 1987: pages 189–99.

Gleason, Jean Berko and S. Weintraub. 'Input Language and the Acquisition of Communicative Competence', in *Children's Language*, vol. 1. Edited by K. E. Nelson, New York: Gardner Press, 1978: pages 171–222.

Gorski, Roger A. 'Sexual Differentiation of the Endocrine Brain and Its Control', in *Brain Endocrinology*, second edition. Edited by Marcella Motla. New York: Raven Press, 1991: pages 71–104.

Groder, Martin G. 'How Couples Can Survive in Changes in One or the Other or Both.' *Bottom Line Personal* (February 1991): page 11.

Gruber, Kenneth and Jacqueline Gaehelein. 'Sex Differences in Listening Comprehension.' *Sex Roles* 5 (1979).

Haas, A. 'Partner Influences on Sex Associated Spoken Language of Children.' *Sex Roles* 7 (1981): pages 925–35.

Harragan, Betty Lehan. *Games Mother Never Taught You – Corporate Gamesmanship for Women*. New York: Warner Books, 1977.

Hawkins, Beth. 'Career Limiting Bias Found at Low Job Levels.' *Los Angeles Times* (9 August 1991): A1, A24.

Henley, Nancy. *Body Politics: Power, Sex and Nonverbal Communication*. Englewood Cliffs, New Jersey: Prentice Hall, 1977.

Henley, Nancy M. 'The Politics of Touch', in *Radical Psychology*. Edited by Phil Brown, New York: Harper & Row, 1973: pages 421–33.

Henley, Nancy M. 'Power, Sex and Non-Verbal Communication' in *Language and Sex: Difference and Dominance*. Edited by Barrie Thorne and Nancy Henley. Rowley, Massachusetts: Newbury House, 1975: pages 184–203.

Henley, Nancy. 'Status and Sex: Some Touching Observations.' *Bulletin of the Psychonomic Society* 2 (1973).

Henley, Nancy and Barrie Thorne. 'Womanspeak and Manspeak: Sex Differences and Sexism in Communications, Verbal and Non-verbal', in *Beyond Sex Roles*. Edited by Alice Sargent. St Paul, Minnesota: West Publishing Company, 1977.

Hirschman, Lynette. 'Analysis of Supportive and Assertive Behavior in Conversations.' Paper presented at meeting of Linguistics Society of America, July 1974.

Hite, Shere. *Woman and Love, A Cultural Revolution in Progress*. New York: Knopf, 1987.

Jacklin, Carol Nagy and Eleanor Maccoby. *Developmental Behavioral Pediatrics*. Edited by M. D. Levine, W. B. Carey, A. C. Crocher and R. T. Gross. Philadelphia: W. B. Saunders Co., 1988.

Jacklin, Carol Nagy and Eleanor Maccoby. *The Psychology of Sex Differences*. Stanford, California: Stanford University Press, 1974.

Jacklin, Carol Nagy and Eleanor Maccoby. 'Social Behavior at Thirty-three Months in Same Sex and Mixed Sex Dyads.' *Child Development* 49 (1978): pages 557–69.

Jourard, Sidney M. and Jane E. Rubin. 'Self-Disclosure and Touching: A Study of Two Modes of Interpersonal Encounter and Their Interrelation.' *Journal of Humanistic Psychology* 8 (1968): pages 39–49.

Kanter, Stefan. 'Sauce, Satire, and Shtick.' *Time* (Fall 1990): pages 62–3.

Kaufman, Margo. 'The Silent Partner.' *Los Angeles Magazine* (4 June 1989): pages 24–5.

Kester, Judy. 'Parade.' *Sex Differences in Human Communication*. Edited by Barbara Westbrook Eakins and Gene R. Eakins. Boston, Massachusetts: Houghton Mifflin, 1978.

Key, Mary Ritchie. 'Linguistic Behavior of Male and Female.' *Linguistics* 88 (1972): pages 15–31.

Key, Mary Ritchie. *Male/Female Language*. Metuchen, New Jersey: Scarecrow Press, 1975.

Kornheiser, Tony. 'Locker-Room Confidential.' *Esquire* (June 1989): pages 97–8.

Kramarae, Cheris. 'Folklinguistics.' *Psychology Today* 8 (June 1974): pages 82-5.

Kramarae, Cheris. *Women and Men Speaking*. Rowley, Massachusetts: Newbury House, 1981.

Kramarae, Cheris. 'Women's Speech: Separate but Unequal?' in *Language and Sex: Difference and Dominance*. Edited by Barrie Thorne and Nancy Henley. Rowley, Massachusetts: Newbury House (1975): pages 43–56.

Kramer, Helen Chmura and Carol Nagy Jacklin. 'Statistical Analysis of Dyadic Social Behavior.' *Psychological Bulletin*, vol. 86, no. 2 (1979): pages 217–24.

Lakoff, Robin. *Language and Women's Place*. New York: Harper Colophon Books, 1975.

Lakoff, Robin. 'You Are What You Say.' *Ms*. 8 (July 1974): pages 63–7.

Lawrence, Barbara. 'Dirty Words Can Harm You.' *Redbook* 143 (May 1974): page 33.

Leary, Mark R. and William E. Snell Jr. 'The Relationship of Instrumentality and Expressiveness to Sexual Behavior in Males and Females.' *Sex Roles* 18 (July 1988): pages 509–22.

Levine, Bettijane. 'Top Women and Their Distinct Style.' *Los Angeles Times* (23 October 1990): page 17.

Lewis, Michael. 'Culture and Gender Roles: There Is No Unisex in the Nursery.' *Psychology Today* 5 (1972): pages 54–7.

Lewis, Michael. 'Parents and Children: Sex Role Development.' *School Review* 80 (1972): pages 229–40.

Lewis, Michael and Linda Cherry. 'Social Behavior and Language Acquisition', in *Interaction, Conversation, and the Development of Language*. Edited by Michael Lewis and Leonard Rosenblum. New York: John Wiley and Sons, 1977: pages 227–45.

Libby, William. 'Eye Contact and Direction of Looking as a Stable Individual Difference.' *Journal of Experimental Research in Personality* 4 (1970).

Ling, D. and A. Ling. 'Communication Development in the First Three Years of Life.' *Journal of Speech and Hearing Research* 17 (1974): pages 159–64.

Lombard, John and Linda Lavine. 'Sex Role Stereotyping and Patterns of Self-Disclosure.' *Sex Roles* 7 (1981).

Lott Dale F. and Robert Somer. 'Seating Arrangements and Status.' *Journal of Personality and Social Psychology* 7 (1967): pages 90–95.

Luchsinger, Richard and Arnold Godfrey. *Voice, Speech and Language*. New York: Constable Press, 1965.

Lynch, Joan A. 'Gender Differences in Language.' *American Speech-Language Hearing Association* (April 1983): pages 37–42.

Maltz, Daniel N. and Ruth A. Borker. *A Cultural Approach to Male–Female Miscommunication in Language and Social Identity*. Edited by John J. Gumperz. Cambridge: Cambridge University Press, 1982: pages 196–216.

Makihara, Kumiko. 'Who Needs Equality?' *Time* (Fall 1990): page 35.

Mathias, Barbara. 'Facing Up to Jealousy.' *Washington Post* (12 November 1985): B5.

Marsh, Peter. *Eye to Eye – How People Interact*. Topsfield, Massachusetts: Salem House, 1983.

Martin, Carol Lynn. 'Attitudes and Expectations About Children with Nontraditional and Traditional Gender Roles.' *Sex Roles* 22, no. 3/4 (1990): pages 151–65.

McGhee, Paul E. *Humor: Its Origin and Development*. San Francisco: W. H. Freeman, 1979.

Merhabian, Albert. *Nonverbal Communication*. Chicago: Aldine Atherton, 1972.

Mitchell, Carol. 'Some Differences in Male–Female Joke Telling', in *Women's Folklore, Women's Culture*. Edited by Rosan A. Jordan and Susan J. Kalcik. Philadelphia: Philadelphia Press, 1985: pages 163–86.

Montagu, Ashley. *The Natural Superiority of Women*. New York: Collier Books, 1978.

Montagu, Ashley. *Touching: The Human Significance of the Skin*. New York: Harper & Row, 1972.

Morrison, Patt. 'Female Officers Unwelcome But Doing Well.' *Los Angeles Times* (12 July 1991): A1, A27, A29.

Morrison, Patt. 'Women Still Finding Bias in Sheriff's Department.' *Los Angeles Times* (13 August 1991): B1, B8.

Naftolin, Frederich. 'Understanding the Basic Sex Differences.' *Science* (March 1981): pages 1263–4.

Naifeh, Steven and Gregory White Smith. *Why Can't Men Open Up?* New York: Clarkson Potter, 1984.

Oakley, Ann. *Sex, Gender and Society*. New York: Harper Colophon, 1972.

Parlee, Mary Brown. 'Conversational Politics.' *Psychology Today* (1979): pages 48–56.

Phillips, Deborah and Robert Judd. *Sexual Confidence*. Boston: Houghton Mifflin, 1980.

Pietropinto, Anthony. *Not Tonight Dear – How to Reawaken Your Sexual Desire*. New York: Doubleday, 1991.

Piercy, Marguerite. *Small Changes*. New York: Doubleday, 1973.

Pine, Devra. 'Tootsie from Dustin – The Sexes.' *In Health* (July 1983): page 66.

Pollitt, Katha. 'Georgie Porgie Is a Bully.' *Time* (Fall 1990): page 24.

Pomerleau, Andree and Daniel Bloduc, Louise Cossetle, Gerard Malcuit. 'Pink or Blue: Environmental Gender Stereotypes in the First Two Years of Life.' *Sex Roles* 22, no. 5/6 (March 1990): pages 359–63.

Puig, Claudia. 'Hollywood Glass Ceiling Cracking?' *Los Angeles Times* (13 August 1991): F1, F4.

Purcell, Pepper and Lisa Steward. 'Dick and Jane in 1989.' *Sex Roles* 22, no. 5/6 (March 1990): pages 177–85.

Ramsay, Rachael. 'Speech Patterns and Personality', in *Language and Sex: Difference and Dominance*. Edited by Barrie Thorne and Nancy Henley. Rowley, Massachusetts: Newbury House, 1975: pages 54–63.

Rose, Suzanna and Irene Hanson Frieze. *Gender and Society* 3 (June 1989): pages 258–68.

Rothman, Allen K. *Hands and Hearts – A History of Courtship in America*. Cambridge, Massachusetts: Harvard University Press, 1987.

Rudolph, Barbara. 'Why Can't a Woman Manage More Like a Woman? Good-bye to the Male Clone, Today's Executive Prefers to Play her Own Rules.' *Time* (Fall 1990): page 53.

Sachs, Jaqueline. 'Cues to Identification of Sex in Children's Speech', in *Language and Sex: Difference and Dominance*. Edited by Barrie Thorne and Nancy Henley. Rowley, Massachusetts: Newbury House, 1975.

Sadker, Myra and David Sadker, Joyce Kaser. *The Communication Gender Gap*. Washington DC: Mid-Atlantic Center for Sex Equality, American University, 1968.

Sadker, Myra and David Sadker. 'Sexism in the Schoolroom of the 80's.' *Today* (March 1985): pages 54–7.

Sears, R. and E. E. Maccoby, H. Levin. *Patterns of Child Rearing*. New York: Harper & Row, 1957.

Segal, Julias and Zelda Segal. 'Little Differences, Snips and Snails and Sugar and Spice: What are Little Boys and Girls Made of?' *In Health* (July 1983): pages 28–31.

Shapiro, Evelyn and Barry M. Shapiro. *The Women Say, The Men Say*. New York: Dell Publishing Co., 1979.

Shapiro, Laura. 'Guns and Dolls.' *Newsweek* (28 May 1990): pages 56–65.

Silberstein, Lisa R. and Ruth H. Striegel-Moore, Christine Timbo, Judith Rodin. 'Behavioral and Psychological Implications of Body Dissatisfaction: Do Men and Women Differ?' *Sex Roles* 19, no. 3/4 (August 1988): pages 23–4.

Silviera, Janette. 'Thoughts on the Politics of Touch.' *Women's Press* (1 February 1972): page 13.

Simpson, Janice C. 'Moving into the Driver's Seat.' *Time* (24 June 1991): page 55.

Spencer, Dale. *Men Made Language*. London: Routledge & Kegan Paul, 1980.

Stechert, Kathryn. *On Your Own Terms – A Woman's Guide to Working with Men*. New York: Vintage Books, 1986.

Strodtbeck, Fred. 'Husband–Wife Interaction Over Revealed Differences.' *American Sociological Review* (1951): pages 468–73.

Swacker, Marjorie. 'The Sex of the Speaker as Sociolinguistic Variable', in *Language and Sex: Difference and Dominance*. Edited by Barrie Thorne and Nancy Henley. Rowley, Massachusetts: Newbury House, 1975.

Tannen, Deborah. *You Just Don't Understand: Women and Men in Conversation*. New York: William Morrow, 1990.

Thorne, Barrie and Nancy Henley. 'Difference and Dominance: An Overview of Language, Gender, and Society', in *Language and Sex: Difference and Dominance*. Edited by Barrie Thorne and Nancy Henley. Rowley, Massachusetts: Newbury House, 1975.

Weitz, Shirley. 'Sex Role Attitudes and Nonverbal Communication in Same and Opposite Sex Interactions.' Paper presented at American Psychological Association, 1974.

Williams, Maureen Smith. 'Women Are Speaking Up, Sort Of.' *McCalls* (March 1981): page 170.

Winitz, Harris. 'Language, Skills of Male and Female Kindergarten Children.' *Journal of Speech and Hearing Research* 2 (1959): pages 377–81.

Ullian, Joseph Alan. 'Joking at Work.' *Journal of Communication* 26 (1976): pages 129–33.

Yarber, Mary Laine. 'First Year Students Are at Greater Risk in On-Campus Rape.' *Los Angeles Times* (25 July 1991): J6.

Zimmerman, Donald H. and Candace West. 'Sex Roles, Interruptions and Silences in Conversation', in *Language and Sex: Difference and Dominance*. Edited by Barrie Thorne and Nancy Henley. Rowley, Massachusetts: Newbury House, 1975.

Zilbergeld, Barney. *Male Sexuality: A Guide to Sexual Fulfillment*. Boston: Little Brown, 1978.

Index

accusation, avoiding 73–4
aggressive women considered
    'bitchy' 140–1
AIDS 121–4
apologising 120–1, 156
appealing to opposite sex 47–8
    by eye and face contact 48–9
arguments during intimacy
    100–2
Arnold, Geoffrey 11
asking for help 74–5
    men vs women 3, 9
assertiveness, female 153–5
attentiveness
    in intimate relationships 94–6
    men vs women 3, 10

bad breath 124–5
Bain, Conrad xi
behavioural patterns, sexual
    differences 24–8
Birdwhistell, Ray 9
blame

avoiding 73–4
self-blame, men vs women 3,
    12
Blank Greifs, Esther 36
Bloomer, Dr H. Harlan ix
body language
    and making love 90–1
    posture that turns your
        partner on 94
    sexual differences 15–17
    in workplace 142–3
body odour 124–5
Boosler, Elaine 74
Borker, Ruth 8, 146
brain development and sex
    differences 31–3
business
    attention paid to in meetings,
        men vs women 2, 5
    poor achievement by women
        viii
    presenting right image
        139–40
    see also work

189

Carousel 35, 67
Charles, Prince of Wales 43–6
children
    different conversational topics
        between sexes 38–9
    environmental influences on
        sex differences in 33–6
    sex differences expectations
        in older 36–8
    sexual equality in raising of 4,
        12
colour differentiation sensitivity
    4–5
communication gap between
    men and women
    closing for good 172–5
communication skills
    how to improve 53–85
        in intimate relationships
            86–133
        during sex 112–17
    to reduce date rape 78–80
    sex differences in ix–xiv
    female *see* female
        communication
    male *see* male communication
compliments, being mean with
    62–4
*Confident Conversation: How to
    Talk in Any Business or Social
    Situation* (Glass) xiii
confrontational, tendency to be,
    male vs female
    in body language 3, 9
    in dealing with problems 4,
        12
Connery, Sean 90–1
conversation
    free-flow 72–3
    subjects to interest men 72
    topics, male vs female 46–7
Coste, Christine de la 33
Costner, Kevin 62
criticism

    of men by women at work
        162–3
    of women by men at work
        162–3
crying
    allowing intimacy 99–100
    men's fear of 66–8
*Cultural Approach of Male-Female
    Miscommunication, The* (Maltz
    and Borker) 8

Darwin, Charles 9
date rape, better
    communication to reduce
    78–80
demanding, male vs female 2,
    7–8
detail, attention to, male vs
    female 3, 5, 9–10
dialogue vs monologue in
    communication 58
Diana, Princess of Wales 43–6
*Differences in Male and Female
    Joke Telling* (Mitchel) 8
Different Strokes xi
diplomacy 124–5
directness of communication in
    business 150
dirty talk 110
divorce, high rate of vii
dominance, conversational 7
Duck, Professor Steven W. 117

Eakins, Barbara and Gene 10
emotion in speech, male vs
    female 3, 11
encouraging men to open up
    71–4
endearment, terms of, as sexist
    at work 158–9
ending an intimate relationship
    126
enthusiastic voice 52–3
environmental influences on sex

differences 33–6
extramarital affairs vii
eye and face contact
   to appeal to opposite sex 48–9
   intimacy through 94–7
   and making love 90–1
eye movement as
   communication skill in
   workplace 144–5

facial language
   sexual differences 17–18
   in workplace 144
failure to communicate and how
   to improve it 53–85
Falk, Peter 6
fantasies, fulfilling sexual 116
fast talkers, male vs female 2, 6
female communication
   to improve relationships with
      men 84–5
      intimate relationships
         132–3
   quiz on 2–4
   quiz answers 4–13
   during sex 106
   what women want to hear
      from men during sex
      107–8
Finch, Steven 112
'First Year Students are at
   Greater Risk in On-Campus
   Rape' (Yarber) 79
Fishman, Pam 11
flirting and sexual harassment
   at work 157–8
free-flow conversation 72–3
Frieze, Irene Hanson 78

Gaehelein, Jacqueline 5
Gallup Polls 1, 8, 12, 13, 60,
   103, 110, 121, 151, 172
gender-specific vs human traits
   173–5

Givens, Dr David 92–3, 142
Gleason, Jean Berko 36
Gorski, Dr Roger 32, 33
gossiping, intimate 119–20
Griffith, Melanie 149–50
Gruber, Kenneth 5
grudges at work 164–6
Gulf War 163

Haas, Dr Adelaide 39, 46
Harlow, Harry 31
Harris Polls 99
head nodding and smiling
   145–6
Hegarty, Mary 112
help, asking for 74–5
Henley, Dr Nancy 6, 8, 10, 11
Hirsham, Lynette 5
Hite, Sherry 68, 172
HIV virus 121–4
Hoffman, Dustin xi
human vs gender-specific traits
   173–5
humour, male vs female 3, 8,
   75–8

improving personal and social
   relationships with opposite
   sex 40–85
information, where to get more
   176–7
interrupting
   men vs women 2, 7
   prevention of
      in others 151–2
      in self 152
intimacy
   arguments during 100–2
   eyes and ears 94–6
   survey 114–16
   teasing during 111–12
   of touch 91–4
intimate relationships
   ending 126

improving communication in 86–133
intimate secrets 118–19
intuition, male vs female 2

Johnson, Magic 123
jokes, sexually offensive 161–2
Jourard, Stanley 10

Kaiser, Susan B. 35
Kester, Judy 7
Key, Mary Ritchie 7
Kramarae, Dr Cheris 39
Kramer vs. Kramer x

Lakoff, Robin x, 4, 6, 7, 8, 10, 11, 153
Landon, Michael 70–1
Language and Sex: Difference and Dominance (Henley) 6
Language and Women's Place (Lakoff) x, 4, 7
letting feelings out 65–6
lively talkers, men vs women 4, 12
looking and listening 59–61
Loving Story 120
Luchsinger, Robert 11

McConnell-Ginetts, Sally 10
McGhee, Paul 8
Madonna 62
making love
communication during, male vs female 3, 8–9
through face and body language 90–1
Malatesta, Professor Carol Z. 34
male communication x
to improve relationships with women 80–3
intimate relationships 127–31
quiz 2–4

quiz answers 4–13
during sex 108
what men want to hear from women during sex 109
Maltz, Dr Daniel 8, 146
Men's Speech to Young Children in Language Gender Society (Gleason and Greifs) 36
Merhabian, Dr Albert 6, 9
Mileikowsky, Dr Gil 30
Mitchel, Carol 8
Montagu, Ashley 4, 173, 174
Moore, Demi 141

nagging, avoiding 73
Naifeh, Steven xii, 68
Natural Superiority of Women, The (Montagu) 4, 173
nature vs nurture 30–1
Naylor, Cecile 33
Not Tonight Dear – How to Reawaken Your Sexual Desire (Pietropinto) 117

opening up, confronting and self-disclosure 68–71
ways to encourage 71–4
orders vs requests 64–5
Ostrum, Dr Maxine 70
outwardly open, men vs women 2

paying compliments, openness in, male vs female 2, 6–7
personal issues, proneness to discuss, men vs women 3, 11
personal life, protecting at work 156–7
Piercy, Marguerite 9
Pietropinto, Anthony 117
Plato, Dana xi
politeness at work 155
posture that turns your partner on 94

projection of voice 51–2
Putz, Linda 160

questions, tendency to ask, men
vs women 4, 12

race, and communication
during sex 105
rape *see* date rape
rejection, fear of, in making love
116–17
requests vs orders 64–5
Richards, Ann 155
Rocky I 99
Rodin, Mary Beth 78
Rose, Suzanna 78
Rosner, Dr Judith 141
Rubin, Jane 10

safe sex 121–4
directness of communication
about 4, 13
Schwarzkopf, General Norman
163
secrets, intimate 118–19
self-blame, men vs women 3, 12
self-defence 80
'Separating the Girls from the
Boys', *In Health* magazine
(Finch and Hegarty) 112
sex, communication during
102–5
'Sex Differences in Listening
Comprehension' (Gruber and
Gaehelein) 5
Sex Talk Differences xi, xiv,
40–3
behavioural patterns 24–8
body language 15–17
evolution of 29–39
facial language 17–18
in intimate relationships 86–9
speech and voice patterns
18–24

in workplace 134–8
Sex Talk Quiz 1–13
Sex Talk Rules vii–viii, xiv
sexual comments, handling at
work 160–1
sexual dysfunction, increased
rate of viii
sexual harassment viii
sexually offensive jokes 161–2
sexually transmitted diseases
121–3
Shucard, Dr David 32
similarity of conversation topics
enjoyed by men and women
4, 13
smiling and head nodding
145–6
Smith, Gregory xii, 68
speech and voice patterns,
sexual differences in 18–24
Stallone, Sylvester 99
Streep, Meryl x
Strodtbeck, Fred 6
Swaaband, Dick 33
Swacker, Marjorie 6

talkers, men vs women as 2, 5–6
Talk to Win (Glass) 51, 110, 151
Tannen, Deborah 9, 12, 74, 156
teasing during intimacy 111–12
Thorne, Barrie 11
Tootsie xi
touch(ing)
intimacy through 91–4
at work, dangers of
misinterpretation 147
*Truth or Dare (In Bed with
Madonna)* 62
Turner, Kathleen 97

'Uhm-mmm' as feedback 148

versatile conversationalists, men
vs women 3, 11

voice
    enthusiastic 52–3
    lowering 149–50
    patterns 148–50
    presenting appealing 49–51
    projecting 51–2
    as sexual barometer 97–9
vocal self-defence 80
vulnerability as sexually
    appealing 99–100

Weaver, Sigourney 150
West, Dr Candice 7, 11, 151
Whittington, Dr H. G. 100
Why Can't Men Open Up?
    (Naifeh and Smith) xii, 68
Williams, Clayton 155
*Women and Love, A Cultural
    Revolution in Progress* (Hite)
    68, 172
Wood, Marion 6
*Word-Play: What Happens When
    People Talk* (Falk) 6
work
    assertiveness, female 153–5
    body language 142–3
    communication 134–71
    criticism of men by women
        162

criticism of women by men
    162–3
crying 163–4
endearment, terms of, as
    sexist 158–9
flirting and sexual harassment
    157–8
grudges 164–6
politeness 155
protecting personal life 156–7
Sex Talk Differences 134–8
sexual comments, handling
    160–1
sexually offensive jokes 161–2
what men need to do when
    working with women 170–1
what women need to do when
    working with men 166–70
Working Girl 149–50
wrong message, communicating
    54–8

Yarber, Mary 79
*You Just Don't Understand: Women
    and Men in Conversation*
    (Tannen) 9, 74

Zimmerman, Dr Donald 7, 11,
    151